ART IN TRANSITION

GUIDELINES FOR TRANSITION YEAR TEACHERS
USING THE NATIONAL GALLERY OF IRELAND

MARIE BOURKE

KEEPER AND HEAD OF EDUCATION

NATIONAL GALLERY OF IRELAND
GAILEARAÍ NÁISIÚNTA NA hÉIREANN

Published in 1998 by
The National Gallery of Ireland
Merrion Square West, Dublin 2

Text copyright © Marie Bourke and the National Gallery
of Ireland, 1998

Supported by The Department of
Education and Science

AN ROINN | DEPARTMENT OF
OIDEACHAIS | EDUCATION
AGUS EOLAÍOCHTA | AND SCIENCE

British Library Cataloguing in Publications Data available

ISBN: 903162814

Front Cover: *A Bouquet of Flowers*,
Jan Van Huysum (1682-1749)

Back Cover: *Fiery Leaves*,
Jack P. Hanlon (1913-1968)

Text Editor: Elaine Campion
Designer: Bill Bolger
Line Drawings: Geraldine O'Neill
Printed in Ireland by: Betaprint

CONTENTS

FOREWORD

In addition to a marvellous capacity to give pleasure and enjoyment, art also has the capacity to enlighten and educate. In this respect it is not only the aspiring artist who can gain knowledge from the study of art, but also the writer, historian or scientist. For students, art has the capacity to complement their work across many disciplines, giving an insight into the life and customs of times gone by, or providing a visual interpretation to a literary subject or historical event or how contemporary society views itself

While most young people have their first introduction to art and museums through their school programmes, not every teenager at second level has the opportunity to study art. At the age of sixteen, however, when young people are in Transition Year, the opportunity may present itself The National Gallery of Ireland has taken this consideration into account and is now providing a new style of conducted tour, ideally suited for such students, based on a themed approach to its collections.

This publication, written by Marie Bourke, Keeper and Head of Education, is designed to help teachers to plan their museum visits for Transition Year students and achieve the maximum benefit from them. This book will help teachers prepare for tours of the collections and provides many ideas, from the simple to the complex, for young people to engage in follow-up work in the classroom.

The publication of *Art in Transition* has been made possible with the assistance of the Department of Education and Science, to whom we are most grateful.

Raymond Keaveney
Director

PREFACE

Art in Transition has been written for Transition Year teachers, who are in the unique position of having access to students who are not working towards a major exam. The Department of Education and Science supports the provision of Transition Year, feeling that because it falls between the Junior and Leaving Certificate, it presents an ideal opportunity for young people to expand their horizons. Transition Year allows students to engage in other aspects of the curriculum such as the arts, and to research specific subjects such as art appreciation, design and the history of architecture. These activities are structured in the form of modules which when combined with placements where students gain work experience in business, sports, industry, educational and cultural institutions, enable them to gain a much broader view of life. This publication will assist teachers to plan and structure modules dealing with the history of art, design and appreciation.

We know that education is a process of lifelong learning. We have seen from recent trends in Europe that education is now regarded less as the transmission of a range of subjects and more as the development of knowledge, skills, understanding and attitudes, with the main objective of achieving fully rounded human beings. This process begins in early childhood and continues throughout every phase of life. It produces a society where human resources are the essential source of social prosperity and individual fulfilment. Transition Year has an important role to play in this process of forming a learning society. The National Gallery of Ireland understands that education is one of its core functions. It is an institution with an extraordinarily rich and international collection available all year round for the public to view, interpret and enjoy. Its Education Service provides an extensive range of activities, enabling adults, young people, families and the community at large, including people with special needs, to gain the maximum benefit from the Collections. School groups form a major segment of the Gallery's audience and much thought is given to designing a wide-ranging programme for schools. This service provides an exciting prospect for any teacher planning a Transition Year.

The Department of Education and Science is pleased to be assisting the National Gallery in several ways; by supporting teacher-training courses through its In Career Development Unit and by distributing the new and innovative educational material which the Gallery is currently producing. We are also pleased to sponsor the book *Art in Transition*, written by Marie Bourke, the Gallery's Keeper and Head of Education, because it provides simple guidelines to help Transition Year teachers make maximum use of their national, regional and local museums. We hope this publication will also encourage teachers and young people to develop a greater appreciation and understanding of their National Gallery.

Micheál Martin, TD
Minister for Education and Science

The National Gallery is aware of the pressure on schools to research and produce programmes that will appeal to the 15-17 age-group that roughly constitute Transition Year. In response to teachers' requests to devise a Transition Year Option, we are offering 'Themed Tours', which involve preparation, follow-up work in the classroom and, we hope, the added feature of being good fun as well as a day's outing for the students!

Art in Transition encourages you to use the Collections for a whole range of project work, by first selecting a tour on a particular theme. The choice is as varied as the works in the Collections, with themes such as Faces and Fashion, History Real and Imagined, Signs and Symbols in Art, Food and Feasting, Music and Dance, or Wildlife. The Guidelines have been structured so that teachers can easily access the information they require. The themed approach to the tour and classroom work can be altered to suit the needs of individual students, and this simple format ensures that all schools can include the option at least once within Transition Year.

Art in Transition embodies the aims and philosophy of Transition Year. These are exciting and challenging times for education. The country is going through a major period of curriculum development and reform, at both Junior and Senior levels. There is a particular emphasis on Transition Year and the unique chance it presents to explore different ways of learning. Transition Year offers students a wonderful opportunity to avail of programmes and modules which build on experiences gained in the Junior Certificate and which will enhance and enrich responses to the Leaving Certificate.

We want students to challenge the subject of art; to look at paintings more closely, to be observant and critically analyse what they see, and thereby to develop a greater understanding and appreciation of art. Our thanks to Maura Clancy, to Paul Doyle and Emer Egan of the In Career Development Unit, and to the Department of Education and Science for supporting this book. We acknowledge the formative role of the Transition Year Support Team, in particular Mary Anne Halton, and also Catherine Bates for the themesheets.

Le gach dhea-ghuí.

Marie Bourke

TRANSITION YEAR THEMED TOURS

The Transition Year Themed Tour is designed for students in the 15–17 age-group. It is greatly helped by good preparation, which enhances the quality of the Gallery visit. The tour takes as a starting point known and familiar themes in art. By focusing on one theme, students develop an appreciation of the variety of ways in which the theme can be communicated, interpreted and understood. Time spent drawing and looking at the works on display forms part of the overall process, which will enable related creative activities to take place back in the classroom.

AIM

The Transition Year Themed Tour aims to create an enjoyable and challenging experience, encouraging students to look and explore, and enabling them to develop a greater understanding and appreciation of art. In so doing it supports the Department of Education and Science's Transition Year Programme.

OBJECTIVES

✳ To develop knowledge and understanding of the history of art
✳ To create awareness of and excite interest in the National Collection
✳ To encourage skills in drawing
✳ To foster skills of observation, critical analysis and appreciation
✳ To promote and encourage creative thought and imagination

A UNIQUE OPPORTUNITY...

For some students this may be their only opportunity to have a direct experience and involvement in an art-related project. For most students the absence of exam pressure should result in their welcoming the chance to engage in art appreciation and drawing. In addition, students who have the benefit of a Transition Year and can avail of projects such as this, should be better equipped to study art for the Leaving Certificate.

GALLERY TUTORS

Themed Tours are conducted by Gallery Guides, all qualified art historians who have the experience necessary to introduce new audiences to the National Collection. They are trained to explain the works of art in simple and uncomplicated language, to deal with mixed-ability groups and to encourage students to express their own views and opinions.

STRATEGIES FOR LEARNING

Transition Year students learn in mixed-ability groups and the tutors will take into account the diverse needs of the various groups. Although the themed worksheets are designed to be used in the Gallery, for the purpose of the Transition Year Tour, teachers may prefer to use them in the classroom, and may choose to use all or part of the worksheet material. If students become particularly interested in a worksheet project, they should be encouraged to carry it out to the best of their ability. All notes, research, sketches and drawings, photographs and written material should be kept for future use.

OUTCOME

A successful outcome depends on adequate preparation of the students, careful attention to the visit, follow-up work and projects in the classroom. On completion of the Transition Year Option students should have a good knowledge and appreciation of part of the Gallery's collection, a sketchbook of drawings and notes, a completed themed worksheet, and at least one of the worksheet projects fully carried out.

TEACHER TRAINING

Transition Year Options require teacher development, which should be accessed through organised In-Service Teacher Training Courses. Transition Year provides an ideal opportunity for teachers and students to pursue further education as a process of lifelong learning. Some preparation work is needed by the teachers to prepare students for the tour, and it is also essential to undertake follow-up work in the classroom in order that students obtain the maximum benefit from the option.

EVALUATION

It is important that teachers undertake a process of evaluation at intervals during Transition Year in order to see if the various options are meeting their students' needs. There are simple methods of assessing the Transition Year Option and one has been listed at the end of Chapter 3. Having carried out an assessment of the Transition Year Option, teachers and students might all then contribute to a full evaluation. The Gallery's Education Department would be interested in the results of these evaluations, and also welcomes any suggestions for further Transition Year Options.

VISITING THE NATIONAL GALLERY

FORWARD PLANNING AND DEVELOPMENT

The National Gallery of Ireland provides education staff and facilities, welcomes school and adult groups and encourages teachers to take part in courses. In so doing, it is supported by the Department of Education and Science and the school curriculum, which encourages the use of resources such as museums and galleries to help develop the expressive and creative abilities of young people. We hope that integrating a well-planned Transition Year Gallery visit with follow-up work and projects in the class-room will provide the potential for learning and making connections in a most rewarding way.

Phone and discuss the proposed visit with education staff. Ask for a Transition Year Pack to be forwarded to you.

Discuss the projected visit with the students, encouraging them to select one of the ten themes available, and listen to any suggestions they may wish to make.

Write to the Gallery's Education Department three weeks in advance of the tour. Indicate the date and time you wish to come, the number and ages of the students, and specify the themed tour and worksheet required. The Department will send confirmation of the themed tour and worksheet requested. The National Gallery is completely accessible to people with disabilities and an Access Guide outlining the services and facilities is available from the Information Desk. Tours are available for people with impaired sight using Tactile Picture Sets (raised reproductions in plastic of ten paintings in the Collection), and tours with interpreters are available for people with hearing impairments.

Good preparation of the student enhances the quality of the visit to the Gallery. Prior to the visit, read the chapter on 'themes' in the handbook *Exploring Art at the National Gallery*, published by the National Gallery and distributed to all schools. Note the approach to using themes explained in the book, and use slides, reproductions, catalogues and the themed

worksheet to help prepare the students – they will enjoy recognising the works on display. Talk to the students about the selected theme; mention (a) some artists who painted using the theme, (b) paintings that illustrate the theme, and (c) projects that could be based on the theme. Encourage the students to bring sketching pads and drawing equipment so that they may learn from the Old Masters.

Before the visit give the students an idea of what to expect. Indicate that the National Gallery is a large building with many beautiful displays. Explain why the objects on display cannot be touched. Mention that good behaviour includes being considerate towards other visitors.

Punctuality is essential for pre-booked tours.

Leave before the students tire. Approximately one to two hours maximum.

Students might want to spend some time in the **Gallery Shop** before leaving, to purchase a book, catalogue, poster, slide, postcard or greeting card as a memento of the visit.

A successful outcome will depend on whether the students enjoyed themselves and want to come back for more.

THE VISIT

It is important to note that the purpose of the Transition Year Themed Tour is to create an enjoyable and challenging experience which will lead students to a better understanding and appreciation of art.

On arrival at the Gallery, register with Reception, letting the Attendant Staff know the name of the party so that they can inform the guide. Ask about arrangements for coats and bags and find out the location of the toilets.
Ask for a floor-plan at the the Information Desk.

Assemble in the Shaw Room. While waiting for the guide, recall the main elements of the Transition Year Tour:

* Take as a starting-point known and familiar themes in art.
* Focus in-depth on one theme so that students can develop an appreciation of the range and variety of ways in which the theme can be communicated, interpreted and understood. This approach can also be applied to collections in many other museums.
* Spend time drawing and sketching in the Gallery rooms to enhance students' knowledge and understanding of what constitutes a work of art.
* Look closely at the pictures on display and at the creativity of others – this process will enable related activities to take place back in the classroom.

Conducted tours of the Gallery are about exploring and developing a sense of discovery. When showing students around the Gallery, the guide will invite questions and initiate discussion. The works of art will be looked at from several different aspects, including the subject, the artist, the period and technique, together with compositional details such as line, shape, form, colour, tone and texture. The guide will encourage the students to express their own thoughts and experiences about the works of art on display.

Curriculum. The class visit can extend beyond the Collection to investigating the architecture of the building. Cross-curricular projects should be encouraged, as well as the disciplines directly served by the Collections, such as Art, Craft and Design, Architecture, Geography, History, Technology and Science and Home Economics. The building and Collections may also be used as stimuli for English, Mathematics, Music and Language development, and for Construction, Environmental and Media Studies.

Practical work. Sketching and taking notes from the paintings cannot be recommended too highly on the Transition Year Tour. When the tour has finished, ask the guide to suggest some areas where the students can draw. Space the students out so that they have adequate room within which to feel comfortable and not interfere with the movement of the public. Be supportive with your comments, especially with mixed-ability students, and encourage them to do as many drawings as time permits.

SOME HELPFUL HINTS

* Ensure everyone involved in the visit is fully briefed.
* Take your time – you don't have to see everything on display.
* It helps to wear comfortable shoes.
* Take a short break – that way no one gets tired.
* Make a head count.
* Know when it's time to stop. The group can always come back again!

'LOOKING' AT PAINTINGS

You do not have to be an art historian or an art expert to look at works of art. By looking, thinking and asking questions, you can discover a great deal, leading to a feeling of personal fulfilment and enrichment. You might first ask yourself: what is the story of the picture? Why did the artist create it? Where was it meant to hang – in a palace, a monastery or a house? Does it fall into any of the themes in the history of art, such as portraits, landscapes, history painting, narratives, mythology, the nude, some of which are included in this book? When was it made and what was going on in the world at that time? What is it painted on? Does it seem well crafted?

Consider your own experience of the work of art. We all have our favourite works of art – objects that stop us in our tracks and take our breath away. How does a work of art affect you? Does it make you feel: happy, sad, angry, calm, frightened or uplifted? Feel free to judge the work. Do you like it? Could you live with it?

Try a different approach with the transition group. First take an easy approach – be a detective! Encourage students to try to work out what kind of people are in the pictures and what jobs they had. Look at some of the portraits. Would they want any of the sitters to be their friend? Compare happy works with melancholy ones, mysterious pictures with obtuse subjects. Explore the pictures, looking for odd, curious and amazing details. Now step up the pace a bit! Look at the pictures to see what people in the past had in their homes, look for evidence of how technology has changed over time, look at how religious beliefs have influenced artists and crafts-people in different cultures.

Adopt a strategy for looking. There are many ways of engaging students in the Collections: ask them to choose a painting which best illustrates *a point of view*, for example, the Nativity was an important subject for artists during the Renaissance and later; identify features which explain *a principle* for example, how animals have adapted to particular habitats, or how designs or details of painting which originated in one part of the world have been copied and adapted elsewhere.

Encourage the students to make choices *individually and in silence*. Then give them an opportunity to explain their choice to the group and describe their ideas and feelings.

Another strategy is to have students work *in small groups*, where they can discuss, for example, pictures that explain a point of view, or plan an imaginary dialogue based on a narrative painting or room-setting.

Students could also find out what *information* is provided on labels and then write their own descriptions and explanations for selected works of art, with *questions* they would like to have answered. They might further consider why particular pictures and pieces of sculpture have been chosen for display.

Reference material

Teachers may wish to answer students' questions by referring to some National Gallery of Ireland/NGI catalogues and books:

NGI illustrated summary catalogue of paintings, 1981

NGI illustrated summary catalogue of drawings, watercolours and miniatures, 1983

NGI illustrated summary catalogue of prints and sculpture, 1988

NGI comprehensive colour illustrated guide. Scala, 1990

NGI colour illustrated guide, 1996

Using the summary catalogues and other catalogues published on the individual schools of painting, you could look up information on the name, date and nationality of the artist, the title of the work, details of its past history and the medium on which it was painted, e.g. canvas, wood panels, paper or board, or further in-depth details about the artist and painting.

Other information may be found in the following reference books:

Cambridge Introduction to Art Series, ranging from the art of Ancient Greece and Rome to twentieth-century art, published by Cambridge University Press

E. H. Gombrich, *The Story of Art*, Phaidon, 1995

E. Grimal, *Dictionary of Classical Mythology*, Penguin, 1996

J. Hall, *Dictionary of Subjects and Symbols in Art*, John Murray, 1996

M. Levey, *From Giotto to Cézanne*, Thames and Hudson, 1990

E. A. Livingstone (Ed.), *Concise Oxford Dictionary of the Christian Church*, Oxford University Press, 1987

P. & L. Murray, *Penguin Dictionary of Art and Artists*, 1991

N. Stangos, *Thames and Hudson Dictionary of Art and Artists*, 1994

S. Woodford, *Looking at Pictures*, Cambridge University Press, 1996

FOLLOW-UP & PROJECT WORK IN THE CLASSROOM

The nature of the follow-up work depends on whether the aims of the visit were understood and on the type of strategies adopted during the visit. What the students have learned and the way in which they have recorded any notes and drawings will have a direct impact on the subsequent work. These practical suggestions will form an integral part of the process of evaluation.

Discussion: Encourage the students to discuss and share the information they gathered in the Gallery; this will enable them to revive the experiences of the visit, listen to others and compare perceptions. How do the students feel about the theme they selected now that they have seen the works on display? Do they feel they saw enough works to understand fully and appreciate the chosen theme? If they visited a different museum, would they be inclined to use this thematic approach? Through discussion and debate, let them explain their likes and dislikes, and in so doing give expression to their thoughts about art. Do they have any views on the way the pictures and sculpture were displayed? How would they have

arranged the displays? Ask them to select one work that affected them from the chosen theme and explain why it had this effect? The excitement felt by students after a visit is a good measure of its success. Teachers need to evaluate the visit to ensure that it met the needs of the students.

Reaffirm the visit by allowing the students to use the oral or written descriptions and explanations which they made during the visit to inspire narrative writing, letter writing, poetry, analytical reports, discussion, drama and music, thereby extending the range and scope of their ideas and knowledge. Another approach is to tabulate data collected, for example, information from labels or architectural details about the building, in a diagram, chart or graph, explaining the findings.

Provide each student with a copy of the themed worksheet and allocate sufficient time to have it completed. Pay particular attention to the highlighted features, including 'Meet the artist', 'Did you know?', 'Subject links' and 'Did you notice?'.

Design projects for Junior and Senior levels are listed separately on the themed worksheets. They provide a good opportunity to explain just why design is so relevant and important to our daily lives. Many people consider design to be the conscious effort of the person to impose meaningful order on life, which in a sense is what all education is about. The problem-solving dimension of design – to plan and implement action to change an existing situation into a preferred one – is the type of approach which has been at the centre of curricular reform in Ireland for over a decade.

What is of benefit to the teacher is the fact that design is a concept through which teaching and learning can establish understanding and generate meaning, and that the practical process of design is central to so many subjects: Art, Craft and Design, Home Economics, Technical Graphics, Mathematics, Science and Construction Studies.

The education philosophy of Transition Year is particularly suited to the development of design awareness and applications. Some teachers may be in a position to encourage students further to get involved in concepts of business and enterprise education, for example, to design, make and market a product. Every teacher should want to help their students understand design because 'engaging in design actively means engaging in the pursuit of excellence.'* This type of approach carried out through problem-solving, practical research, personal evaluation and scrutiny applies equally to all the subjects in the curriculum.

Select one of the 'Design Projects': The choice could range from: designing a two-page tourist brochure on transport, travel and tourism in Ireland; an outdoor nature study based on a tree – taking tracings from the bark of a tree, noting the shape of the branch and the outline of a leaf; making a brochure to educate people about poverty; creating full-scale costumes for circus performers; even producing a small model for a life-size public sculpture to reflect the theme of peace. Suggest that when the students begin to consider how they will approach the project, they use the following helpful guidelines:

Design in Education, edited by I. McCarthy and G. Granville, NCAD & NCCA, 1997.

1. Use their skills of observation, enquiry and visualisation.
2. Identify the problem and begin the process of researching and solving it.
3. Develop the skill of analysis and evaluation.
4. Become critically aware and develop an appreciation of the pattern and shapes, the texture and colours, the systems and processes in the natural, human and built environment.

The students should consider all the research gathered in the Gallery, including notes, written material, drawings, designs, pastel and paintings in planning their project. All the preliminary drawings and research are relevant. In the final analysis the ability of the student to illustrate and explain all the stages in the process of creating the project is as important as the completed project itself.

You may find that the students have learned so much in the various stages of designing a brochure, for instance, that you could further ask them to plan an advertising campaign to launch the brochure, and design a poster for the advertising campaign.

Classroom Display: the teacher could set the students the task of preparing a classroom display using some of the notes and drawings gathered in the Gallery and reflecting some of the display techniques observed during the course of the visit. This could involve a small sub-group being nominated to select the works for display, another group to mount the works on coloured board, and the remainder to hang and label the drawings and paintings. The teacher could use the display to illustrate how the students have acquired and developed their knowledge and understanding of one aspect of the history of art through direct experience of the Collections in the National Gallery.

'Floor-Plan' Exhibition: A good exercise to carry out with the students, subsequent to the Classroom Display, would be to suggest creating floor-plans of one of the rooms in the Gallery, noting public access, lighting and colour schemes, the hanging of the paintings and display of sculpture. Exhibit all the floor-plans on the walls of the classroom. Discuss the plans and allow the students express their own perceptions and ideas. Did they like the decoration of the rooms? Were the paintings well hung and displayed to their best advantage? Did the lighting influence the hanging of the paintings? Were the labels clear and legible, too brief or about right? Were people with disabilities and special needs adequately catered for? Was the sculpture well positioned? Do they mind some objects being placed behind glass – do they know of any other way to protect them against damage? Conclude the discussion by encouraging each student to explain his or her own design. Finally, suggest they pay another visit to the National Gallery in their own time. Encourage them on this occasion to look critically at the works of art on show and at the rooms they are displayed in. Do they agree that the Transition Year Option of theme-based tour, worksheet, project and discussion has enabled them to be more critical in appraising their surroundings,

resulting in a much greater appreciation of their National Gallery.

Project Rationale: All of the themes listed in this book could be pursued further if there was flexibility in the Transition Year Timetable. The teacher could suggest that the students structure their approach to the Transition Year Tour Option, e.g. what is the aim of the tour? what do they feel should be the content of the projects? what resources do they feel they need? When the tour and project have been completed, are they in a position to evaluate the overall process and results? Do they see the theme they have chosen as having a social and community element? Does it have a European dimension? Does the theme have a business context? Is it possible to link in with multimedia? These are just a few ways of encouraging the students to think in a broader context about the theme they have chosen. Perhaps they have an idea for a theme that is not on the list!

A simple way to assess the Transition Year Option is to provide a number of headings under which students can give their views and comments. A sample sheet might read:

TRANSITION YEAR OPTION ASSESSMENT

Student's Name:...

Transition Year Option: ....

Circle the relevant comment:

Was the Gallery Transition Year Themed Tour enjoyable? yes/no Beneficial: yes/no

* Was the Gallery Transition Year Themed Tour enjoyable? yes/no Beneficial: yes/no
* Did you spend time drawing in the Gallery? Yes/no
* Did you find this experience difficult/enjoyable/constructive/boring/very useful?
* Did taking part in the tour make you want to visit the Gallery again? Yes/no
* Did you complete the themed worksheet? Yes/no
* Was it hard/tough enough/average/easy?
* Did you do any of the worksheet projects? Yes/no
* Would you recommend the Transition Year Tour Option for future classes? Yes/no

Answer the following in the space provided:

Describe the project you undertook.

If you could change one aspect of the Transition Year Option, what would it be?

Express in your own words what was the value of the Gallery Tour.

Teacher's Notes

Rate on a 1-20 basis
1.   Performance on the Gallery Themed Tour:
2.   Quality of drawing in the Gallery:
3.   Completed the themed worksheet?   on time?
4.   Standard of themed worksheet project completed:
5.   Presentation of the project work, research and notes:

Further Comments: ---

Date:

Teacher's Name:

Note: These Assessment Sheets should be compiled and used to chart a student's progress through Transition Year. They are also useful to note particular options or modules that appear too easy, too difficult, or where there is room for improvement.

SENIOR CYCLE THEMED WORKSHEETS AND ACTIVITY SHEETS

1. FACES AND FASHION

2. SCENES FROM THE LIFE OF CHRIST

3. FOOD AND FEASTING

4. HISTORY REAL AND IMAGINED

5. LAND AND SEA

6. EVERY PICTURE TELLS A STORY

7. WEIRD AND WONDERFUL WILDLIFE

8. MUSIC AND DANCE

9. TOWN AND COUNTRY

10. SIGNS AND SYMBOLS

Post-Primary Worksheet 1
Faces and Fashions

National
Gallery *of*
IRELAND

In the Spanish Rooms, find:
Doña Antonia Zárate,
Francisco de Goya
(1746-1828)

Ten years before he painted
this portrait, Goya went
completely deaf after a
serious illness.
How might this have
changed his attitude to life?

Do you think it might have
affected his paintings too?

Doña Zárate, the lady in
this painting, was a famous
Spanish actress. What kind
of parts do you think she
would have played, judging
by this portrait?

Why do you think so?

Name some films or
characters in films you have
seen that you think Doña
Zárate would be right for.

Draw a scene from a film or play around Doña Zárate.
Put in the words the characters are saying, if you like.

Meet the artist
Francisco de Goya was principal painter to Charles IV, King of Spain. He was
also a very active printer; 'The Disasters of War' were his best-known etchings

---

Subject link: English
Write a short sketch with
Doña Zárate *as the main*
character, sitting on her sofa.

Did you know?
Sir Alfred and Lady Beit donated this picture, along with other masterpieces
from Russborough House, to the National Gallery. Sir Alfred successfully
proposed to his wife under this painting.

In the French Rooms, find:
Marie-Julie Bonaparte, Queen of Spain, with
her two daughters, Zenaïde and Charlotte,
Baron François Gérard (1770-1837)

Did you know?
Julie Bonaparte, of Irish descent, was married to
the Emperor Napoleon's brother Joseph. Her huge
dowry saved the brothers from poverty, and helped
to start their political careers.

Did you know?
After the fall of Napoleon, the Bonaparte family
had to emigrate quickly. In the rush, Prussian
soldiers slashed this painting. Luckily the artist was
alive and able to repair the damage, and the
painting was returned to the family.

Meet the artist
Baron Gérard trained under another French artist,
Jacques-Louis David. Gérard was one of
Napoleon's principal painters.

Julie Bonaparte was French, as was her husband, and
so was Gérard, the man who painted this scene. She
became Queen of Spain when her husband was appointed King by his brother Napoleon.

Describe the differences in ladies' fashion between Spain and France, based on these paintings of Doña Zárate and
Julie Bonaparte:

Spanish	French

Describe the differences in appearances between the Spanish and French women:

Spanish	French

Describe the differences in painting styles between the two pictures – they were both painted around 1808:

	Spanish	French
Colour		
Line		
Light/shade		
Attention to detail		
Any other difference		

Design project
Senior level: Design a series of election campaign posters.
Junior level: Design a book cover for one of these titles: 'Kings and Queens', 'The Clothes They Wore', or 'The
Famous Family'. *Consider lettering in the overall designs.*

In the Dutch Rooms, find:
Jeronimus Tonneman and His Son Jeronimus,
Cornelius Troost (1696-1750)

This is the third portrait you have looked at. Why do you think people want to have their portraits painted?

Who do you think each of these portraits were for (family, friends, public, etc)?

	Intended audience
Dona Zarate	
Julie Bonaparte	'
Jeronimus Tonneman	

Are there any other reasons why portraits are painted?

The background, costumes and objects included in a portrait are usually carefully chosen because of what they say about the people.
Why do you think Jeronimus Tonneman wanted such beautiful carvings, furniture and sculptures around him?

Describe the differences between Jeronimus and his son. Look at every aspect of the portrait for clues – their faces, poses, costumes and even the furniture.

Jeronimus Junior	Jeronimus Senior

If you were to paint someone well-known in Ireland today, who would you portray? How would you portray them? What would you include to explain who the figure is?
Draw a rough sketch of your ideas below.

Did you know?
The plaster carvings and the statue in this painting are included as warnings against vanity and pride. Moral lessons like these were a feature of Dutch 17th-century painting.
Do you think they were included as a suggestion to the subjects to mend their ways, or might the artist have been taunting Jeronimus with these carvings? Discuss.

Senior level project
When you get back to the artroom, do a large colour variation on this modern celebrity portrait. Using any materials you like, paint a portrait of a modern celebrity. You could make it a genuine portrait, or you could choose objects, clothes etc to make fun of the person. Use photographs to help you with the face.

Meet the artist
Cornelius Troost was a Dutch portrait painter. He was also involved in the theatre as an actor and as a painter of stage sets.

In the English Rooms, find:
King George III,
John Van Nost the Younger
(1712-1780)

This sculpture is also a portrait. Do you find looking at this sculpture different from looking at the paintings?
Explain:

Which do you think has more effect on you as you look at it – painting or sculpture?

Why?

George III was made King of England in 1760. Why do
you think he decided to wear a Roman general's
uniform for his portrait, instead of royal robes?

Draw some of the details and different textures from
the sculpture below. Note the detail of the armour, and
the lion's head on the belt and sandals.

Junior level project
*Using coloured paper, cut out shapes of figures of
different heights. Make the smallest about a
quarter of the size of the biggest, and make the
others sizes in between. Stick these figures onto a
page, with the biggest figure at the bottom of the
page, the smallest at the top, and the others in the
middle. This gives the impression that the small
people at the top are further away than the bigger
people at the front. Then draw the scene around
them, or try doing it in collage.*

Meet the artist
John Van Nost the Younger came from an Irish family
of sculptors, who had already created three royal
portrait sculptures in Ireland.

Did you know?
George III's reign was a difficult one for England.
During his time America fought and won independence
from England, there was a rebellion in Ireland, and he
himself suffered from serious mental illness.

Post-Primary Worksheet 2
Scenes from the Life of Christ

National Gallery of IRELAND

In the Icon Rooms, find:
Virgin and Child,
Paolo Uccello (1397-1475)

This painting was done over 500 years ago. Uccello was fascinated with geometry, and how basic shapes work together. What geometric shapes do you see in the painting?
Draw them in this box. Leave out the details, just draw shapes like triangles, etc.

The lines used for the Virgin Mary are different to those used for the baby. How are they different?

What moods do the different lines give the figures?

Do you think the artist is more concerned with showing the feeling between the mother and child, or with presenting the two images? Why do you think this?

Look at the clothes and the architecture. Do these look like they belong to the year 0, or to 15th century Italy?

Complete the above drawing, putting the two figures against a background view of the time.

Meet the artist
Paolo Uccello was painting in Italy at the time of the Early Renaissance. He was particularly interested in perspective and geometry.

Did you notice?
Uccello painted a false picture frame at the bottom of the canvas, and made the baby's knee come out over it. It makes the infant look very lively.

Did you know?
A dark veil was once painted over the figure of the Virgin Mary by another, later artist, possibly because the realistic poses of the figures weren't thought to be holy enough. The veil was removed when the painting was restored in the 1960s.

Project
The paintings in this worksheet show Christ at different stages of his life, from early childhood onwards. Make your own series of portraits based on your life. Find photos of yourself at different ages, and pick four to base your drawings or paintings on. Details like clothes are important, because fashions show when the painting was done. The clothes in these religious paintings show that Christ lived a long time ago. Make the paintings sufficiently small to stick them all onto one big page when you're finished. You could use the same procedure to do a portrait of someone else too.

In Room 11, find:
A Scene from the childhood of Christ in Egypt,
James Tissot (1836-1902)

Meet the artist
James Tissot, a French artist, painted scenes of upper-class life until 1882, when he claimed to have seen a religious vision. He began to paint religious scenes, executing some 800 in the last twenty years of his life.

Tissot portrays Christ as a child. Unlike Uccello, he was very interested in history, and to make sure he got all the historical details right he spent six months in Egypt and Palestine.

Draw a section of the background in the box below. Beside it draw the view from your bedroom or classroom window.

Egypt	Ireland

Compare the two under the headings below:

. .	Egypt	Ireland
Colours		
Light		
Shapes		
Vegetation		

Tissot carefully researched the life and times of Christ. Do you think he knew how a small boy would have lived?

Draw some toys, games or amusements that Jesus might have played with as a young boy in the box below.

Did you know?
This scene is set across the river from where it was believed that Pharaoh's daughter found Moses. In this way Tissot links the Old and New Testaments.

Subject link: History and English
Jesus and the Virgin Mary are shown living their lives as ordinary people, among the women drawing water from the river. Think how much social customs have changed since people used to go in groups to fetch water – now all we have to do is turn on a tap. Write a short story based on changes in lifestyle through the years.

In the Flemish Room, find:
Christ in the House of Martha and Mary,
Jan Brueghel (1601-1678) and Peter Paul Rubens (1577-1640)

The Gospel of St Luke tells us that on one occasion Christ visited Martha and Mary. While Martha was busy with household chores, Mary sat and listened to Christ's words. Martha complained that Mary wasn't helping, and Christ replied that Mary was right to be concentrating on his teachings, rather than on the concerns of this world.

In this painting two artists worked on the same canvas. Rubens painted the figures, and Brueghel did the landscape and animals.

How can you tell that they were painted by different artists?

Did you know?
Christ in the House of Martha and Mary is a scene usually shown in a kitchen setting, but Brueghel and Rubens moved it outdoors to concentrate more on the landscape.

Project
Do a shared painting of some aspect of the Life of Christ with another student. Decide on the story, and on what you both want to illustrate. Divide the subject between you, and start painting. You might need to discuss the project as you go along. When you have finished, see if you can tell that it was by two different people. Are there any differences between your styles?

In this painting Christ has grown up to be a man, and has started his public teaching. Christ is rarely shown in art as a teenager. How might he have looked if he were born two thousand years later? In the box below, draw him as a teenager in the year 2015, surrounded by his favourite things.

Did you know?
Most of the animals in the painting symbolise something, e.g. the dog beside Martha represents loyalty and faithfulness.

Meet the artists
Peter Paul Rubens from Flanders (now Belgium) was famous for painting a wide range of subjects: landscapes, portraits and religious scenes.
Jan Brueghel, also Flemish, came from a famous family of artists and painted mainly landscapes and narratives (paintings of stories).

In the French Rooms, find:
The Lamentation over the Dead Christ,
Nicolas Poussin (1594-1665)

Poussin's depiction of the dead Christ before burial almost looks like a relief sculpture rather than a painting, with its simple geometric shapes.
Do you think he paints in a similar way to Rubens and Brueghel? Explain why / why not:

Which do you prefer? Why?

Meet the artist
Nicolas Poussin was a French painter interested in antiquity who spent most of his life in Rome. He was the finest history painter of the 17th century.

Did you notice?
Each figure has been painted in a separate, strong colour. Poussin possibly did this to show how each person was distinct from the others, reflecting their private sorrow at Christ's death.

Did you notice?
On the tree beside the entrance to the tomb there are two sprouting shoots – these symbolise regrowth after the Resurrection.

Describe the emotions in this painting:

How has Poussin created these feelings?

Name four different things in this painting which add to the mood:

How is the lighting important to the painting?

The artist was clearly affected by this scene - look at how he has painted the distraught figure of the Virgin Mary. In what way would you have been affected if you had been present at this event?

Design projects
Senior level: Think about designing an advertising campaign based on the subject of beliefs or religions. How would you portray them?
Junior level: Design a book cover based on one of these themes: 'Birth and death', 'brightness and darkness'.

Imagine that, having taken Christ down from the cross, his friends organise a traditional funeral for him. Write a funeral speech in the space below for the Virgin Mary, looking back on Christ's life (you could use the other three paintings on the worksheet for inspiration).

Post-Primary Worksheet 3
Food and Feasting

National Gallery *of*
IRELAND

In the Dutch Rooms, find:
A Banquet Piece,
Willem Claesz Heda
(1593/4-1680/2)

> *Meet the artist*
> *Willem Claesz Heda* was a very popular still-life painter in Holland in the 17th century.

Describe 5 items from **A Banquet Piece** in this chart. Try to find exactly the right words.

	How would they feel to touch?	How is the light on the object painted?
Metal Jug		
Ham		
Tall Wineglass		
White Cloth		
Bread Roll		

Do you think this looks like the leftovers of a real meal, or do you think the artist set up this scene to show off his skills as a painter? Explain:

Heda has used a variety of brushstrokes to create the effect of different tones. There are other ways to create these effects: by hatching, cross-hatching and stippling.
Use a pencil to make value scales from dark to light in the boxes below:

	Dark → → → → → → Light
Hatching	
Cross-hatching	
Stippling	
Blending	

Use this table as a reference when drawing in tone.

Senior level project
At home, take a piece of fruit and make a detailed drawing of it. Then cut it in half and draw it from different angles. Use coloured pencils or pastels to colour it. Leave these pieces of fruit somewhere safe and dry. After a few days take out the fruit and draw it again. You will be surprised at the difference between the two drawings.
If you feel really enthusiastic about the project, you could keep drawing the fruit after intervals of a few days, and build up a collection of studies of the fruit as it decays.

Did you know?
This kind of pewter jug is called a 'Jan Steen' because the painter Steen used it so often in his paintings. Have a look at *The Marriage Feast at Cana* by Steen, which contains some jugs like this one.

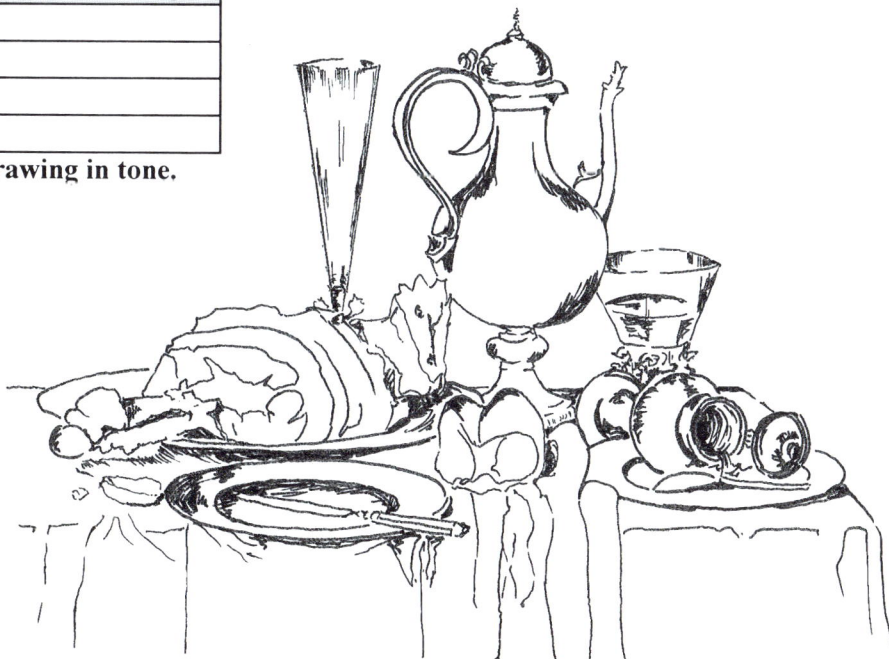

In the Spanish Rooms, find:
Still Life with a Mandolin,
Pablo Ruiz Picasso (1881-1973)

Picasso's interest, in *Still Life with a Mandolin*, is very different to Heda's. It is much harder to describe the textures of the objects in Picasso's painting because the artist concentrates on colours and patterns instead.

Picasso felt free not to follow the traditional rules of perspective and proportion. Instead of making the objects realistic, he has deliberately flattened individual elements because he is more interested in making decorative patterns on the picture surface. It sounds difficult but the effect is spectacular.

Did you notice?
Is the object on the left of the painting a fruit bowl? Is the white mask-like shape the inside of the bowl? Is the green object a fruit or a fish? The red patterned section may be a huge strawberry. What do you make of the objects in the picture?

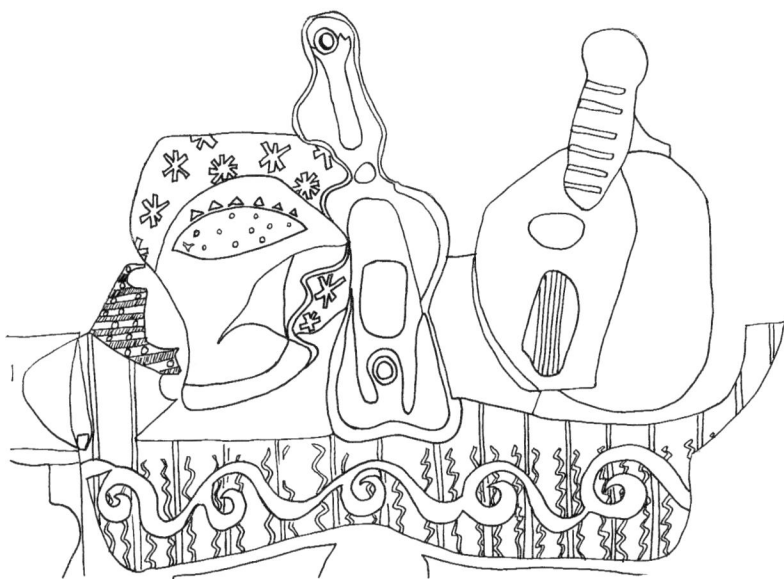

Imagine how Picasso might have painted people, if this is how he painted a still life. Draw some Picasso-style people sitting around this table.

Make a pattern-chart below with four of Picasso's patterns. In the next chart, draw your own patterns.

Use these to start a pattern reference collection – cut patterns out of newspapers and magazines, and draw any you see around you. You can use these for ideas when designing repeat patterns.

Subject link: English
Write a paragraph on the difference in style between Picasso and Heda. Draw one object from each painting at the top of the page, and write the paragraph underneath. Describe their styles as clearly as possible – imagine a blind person trying to picture them from your description.

In the Spanish Room, find:
Kitchen Maid with the Supper at Emmaus,
Diego Velázquez de Silva (1599-1660)

Look at Velázquez' ***Kitchen Maid with the Supper at Emmaus***. Put your hand over your eye to cover the scene in the window behind. This was how the painting looked until 1933, when the background was uncovered during cleaning.

Use your imagination to compare and contrast the *before* and *after* versions of the painting in the table below:

	Before cleaning	After cleaning
Focus point		
Balance		
Mood		
Meaning/message		
Other comments		

The Supper at Emmaus.

Two disciples were walking along the road to Emmaus when they met a man walking in the same direction. They started talking to him. They invited the stranger to eat with them, and it was only when he broke the bread at supper that they recognised that he was the risen Christ, but by then he had vanished.

Why do you think Velázquez has made the maid with the still life so much bigger and more important than the religious scene?

Here is a line drawing of the scene as it would have looked if the painter had decided to place them the other way around. Which effect do you like better? Why?

> **Meet the artist**
> *Diego Velázquez* became court painter to the Spanish King Philip IV. He painted many portraits of the king and his family, as well as still lifes.

Design project
Junior level: *Make a dramatic poster based on one of these themes:* celebrations, food, the senses, inside/outside.
Senior level: *Base a project on one of these themes, then design a corresponding advertising campaign:* the environment, parks and green areas, pollution, recycling.

Did you know?
The Moorish (North African) kitchen maid is included as a reminder that many slaves in Spain at this time were converted to Christianity.

Did you know?
The combination of still life and a scene from daily life in a kitchen setting is called a *bodegón*. These were very popular in Spain at this time, and the inclusion of the religious scene would have raised the humble bodegón to a higher level.

In the Italian Rooms, find:
Party Feasting in a Garden,
Giovanni Baptista Passeri (1610-1679)

Passeri's *Party Feasting in a Garden* was also overpainted at one time during its history. The fountain on the right, the statue on the left, and the urn in the centre were all painted over with trees or bushes, which were removed in 1983 during cleaning.

Do you think someone has a right to change a work painted by another artist? Explain why/why not:

During cleaning, do you think any overpainting should be removed? Why/why not?

These are difficult questions that require some thought, and they apply equally to sculpture and architecture.

Subject link: Speech and Drama
Organise two teams for a debate on the subject: 'Art and architecture should be allowed to change over time – the original is a building-block, not a finished work.'

What do you think is the mood of the people in this painting?

Invent a funny short story about what happened to the people at the table to explain their mood. Write a brief outline of the plot below.

Did you know?
This painting may be a *memento mori* (reminder of death) – a warning that life is short. The inclusion of classical sculpture is a reminder of a great society that also came to an end. This may explain the serious faces of the revellers.

Project
Do a series of drawings to show the lifespan of a fruit or a vegetable. You could show it growing, ripening, being picked, sold, bought and prepared as food, being eaten, and you could even show its progress through the digestive system! Go to the shop to buy the fruit or vegetable, take pictures or draw in the shop, then prepare the food for eating, drawing it at different stages of production. Then start to eat it, again drawing it at different stages. Don't forget to use colour and texture carefully.

Post-Primary Worksheet 4
History Real and Imagined

National
Gallery *of*
IRELAND

In the Italian Rooms, find:
Judith with the Head of Holofernes,
Andrea Mantegna (1432-1506)

This picture looks more like marble than a painting, because it is painted in *grisaille*, a technique using only tones of grey, to imitate relief stone carving.
Why do you think the artist decided to create this effect? Do you think it might be because he is trying to recreate a scene from history, or do you have a different theory?

This story comes from the Old Testament. Judith was a beautiful, rich widow whose country was invaded by a much bigger army. To save her city she pretended to desert it, and went into enemy territory. She charmed the general of the enemy army, Holofernes, and while he slept, she cut off his head with his own sword. Her servant helped her to bring the severed head home, and when the enemy discovered their general dead, they retreated.

> **Meet the artist**
> *Andrea Mantegna*, an Early Italian Renaissance painter, was fascinated by antique sculpture which he used for inspiration in his pictures.

Describe the headdress and/or hairstyles of the three figures in the painting:

Judith	
Her servant	
Holofernes	

Change their hairstyles on this drawing, making them more modern – you could even give them punk hairstyles! Does this make the whole scene look more up-to-date? Describe the new effect:

Do you think that hairstyles and costumes are important in history paintings? Why?

When you get home, find some old family photos and look at how the fashions have changed. Make a year-by-year fashion chart, showing the type of clothes and hairstyles that were fashionable every year since you were born.
Use colour for maximum effect, and don't be afraid to exaggerate the styles.

> **Did you notice?**
> The foot of Holofernes' body can be seen sticking out of the tent on the left.

In the English Rooms, find:
The Dublin Volunteers on College Green, 4th November 1779,
Francis Wheatley (1747-1801)

The Irish Volunteers were formed to defend Ireland against a threatened invasion from France. They were also used as a lever to get concessions from Britain in the areas of parliament and trade. They held an annual gathering to commemorate the birthday of King William III, whose statue can be seen in front of Trinity College in this picture. The painting shows a large and impressive gathering which they held in 1779, which Wheatley saw when he was in Dublin.

Do you think Wheatley was interested in the detail of this scene?
Explain:

> *Meet the artist*
> *Francis Wheatley*, an English artist, painted many different kinds of subjects, including portraits, landscapes and interiors. He spent four years in Ireland.

People all through the years have felt the need to record historical events – in songs, poems, stories, paintings, sculpture and photography. Can you think of any songs (traditional or pop songs) or poems about historical events? Name some:

Pick one of the events they describe and draw it in the box on the right. Include lots of detail, as Wheatley did.

> *Did you know?*
> The statue of William III on his horse was regarded as insulting by many people, because of his position with his back to Trinity College, a centre of learning. The statue was knocked over by an explosion in 1836, and finally removed in 1929.

> **Subject link: Geography**
> *If you live in Dublin, walk down Dame Street towards Trinity College. How have the architectural features, cityscape and city life changed since 1779?*
> *Do a quick sketch of the same view as Wheatley saw, and see where the differences lie.*

In the Italian Rooms, find:
The Visit of the Queen of Sheba to Solomon,
Lavinia Fontana (1552-1614)

Meet the artist
Lavinia Fontana was one of the first of many successful Italian women artists. Most of her commissions came from Italian nobles, and she has painted some of their portraits in this picture. Solomon is probably a portrait of the Duke of Mantua, and the Queen of Sheba is probably his wife, Elenora de' Medici.

Describe the differences between the outfits worn by people in Dublin in 1779 (as seen in **The Dublin Volunteers**), and by those in Italy around 1600, as shown in this painting:

Ireland		Italy	
Men	*Women*	*Men*	*Women*

The scene in this picture represents another story from the Old Testament. The Queen of Sheba had heard a lot about how wise Solomon was, so she decided to travel to see him for herself and to ask him some hard questions. On arriving at his palace she presented him with gifts.

Subject link: English
What kind of questions would you like to ask someone who was very wise? Write a page of really tough questions to put to Solomon when you get back to school – jot a few here to start you off. You could ask questions you've always wanted to know the answers to.

Travel was quite difficult many years ago. What kind of hardships would the travellers have had to endure on their journey to Solomon?

Most of the figures in this painting, male and female, are wearing beautiful costumes and jewellery. In the box opposite, do some quick sketches of ideas for jewellery designs that could be worn today, by men or women, inspired by this painting.

Project development
When you get back to the classroom, produce full-size colour drawings of two of your ideas for pieces of jewellery.

Did you know?
Leandro Bassano also painted a version *of The Visit of the Queen of Sheba* – his picture is also in the Italian Rooms. Find it and see which painting you prefer.

In the Spanish Room, find:
The Prophet Elias, Patron of the Carmelites, Overthrowing the False Prophets of Baal,
Juan Alonso Villabrille Y Ron (?1663-1732)

Elias was a Christian prophet in Israel. The Queen of Israel had become a believer in the pagan fertility god, Baal, as had many others. Elias challenged the prophets of Baal to prove that their god existed, and when they couldn't, he killed them.

Do you think that this sculpture is more or less dramatic than Fontana's painting? Explain why:

Meet the artist
Juan Alonso Villabrille y Ron, a Spanish sculptor, produced religious works full of realism and emotion.

Draw an unusual view of the sculpture in the above space. Try sitting or kneeling – it will give you a different view than standing. When you're finished, decide which you prefer – your view or the one drawn here. Why?

You can walk around a piece of sculpture because it is three-dimensional, but you can only look at one side of a painting, because it is a flat surface. Do you think that looking at this scene from so many different angles adds to its effect? Explain:

This statue was made of painted wood with glass eyes. Imagine it in a dark church, lit by flickering candles. Do you think it would look more or less impressive?

The placing of this sculpture in a brightly-lit room in the Gallery gives a very different effect. What do you think are the reasons for, and against, having it in a Gallery, compared to its original location?

For	Against

Design projects
Junior level: Design a poster for a horror film. Invent the name of the film, and make some areas of the poster three-dimensional, to add to the scary effect.
Senior level: Produce a small model for a life-sized public sculpture to show your ideas about one of the following themes: war, famine, peace.

Did you know?
Elias challenged the prophets on Mount Carmel, and as a result he became the patron of the Carmelite order. That's why he is shown wearing the brown Carmelite habit in this sculpture, covered in a goatskin cloak.

Subject link: Speech and Drama
Organise two teams for a debate on this motion: 'That art should be displayed in its original location.'

Do you think that these four works have given you a sense of history and the passage of time? Why / why not?

Post-Primary Worksheet 5
Land and Sea

N
G I

National
Gallery *of*
I R E L A N D

In the Dutch Rooms, find:
The Castle at Bentheim,
Jacob Isaacksz. van Ruisdael (1628-1682)

When you think of the landscape in Holland, what details come to mind?

Can you see any of these details in this painting?

Are there any mountains in Holland?
Do you think the artist was painting this mountain as he saw it, or as he wanted it to be?

Why do you think he did this?

Did you know?
The artist painted this castle at Bentheim, in Westphalia, near the border between Holland and Germany, over fourteen times!

Above is a line drawing of the foreground of this picture. Draw in the hill and the castle, but this time make them much smaller. What effect does this have on the impact of the painting?

Did you notice several small figures in the painting? There are two on the hill, and one near the river. Can you see any others?

Why do you think the artist made the figures so tiny compared to the trees and the castle?

What kind of feeling does this create in the painting?

Does anything else add to this feeling – if so, what?

In the Irish Rooms, find:
Ideal Landscape,
Thomas Roberts
(1748-1778)

Meet the artist
Thomas Roberts was the most gifted Irish landscape painter in the second half of the 18th century. Unfortunately he died of TB at the age of thirty.

Do you think this painting represents a real view, or an invented or idealised one? Why?

This idealisation is one similarity between this painting and the last one. Are there any other similarities? Describe them:

Do you think that the river is important in this painting? Why?

Draw the basic structure of the *Ideal Landscape* in this box, but leave out the river.
Now do you see why the river is important? It leads the eye from the foreground (front) of the painting into the distance.

Do you notice any difference between the colours Roberts used in the foreground of the painting, and those in the background?
Fill in this table with the colours he used for the two areas.

Foreground	Background

What effect does this difference in colour create in the picture?

Sketch the blocks of colour which Roberts used in this box – no lines, just colours. Try using these colours next time you paint a landscape, and see if they work for you.

Did you know?
Like the French painter *Claude Lorrain*, Roberts was interested in painting ideal and classical landscapes. As you walk through the French Rooms on your way to the last painting on this worksheet, look for ***Juno confiding Io to the Care of Argus*** by Claude Lorrain, and see how similar his landscape is to Roberts' idealised view.

In the Irish Rooms, find:
Landscape with Rocks,
Roderic O'Conor
(1860-1940)

The colours in this painting
are very different to those in
the last one. Suggest a few
reasons why:

Colour this line drawing in
O'Conor's style.

Can you feel the heat in this scene? How has the artist created this feeling?

This is the first painting on this worksheet which doesn't include people. In the
previous paintings the figures helped to give a sense of scale to the scenes.

Do you find it difficult to work out the scale of the objects in this picture, or are
there any other clues?

In the box below, redraw the rough lines of this view and add in some figures to
show what scale you think the scene might have.

Subject link: English
Imagine that you are Gulliver on his travels, or Alice in
Wonderland. Write a paragraph describing the world as
a huge area, seen by someone really tiny, and then write
a second one describing a microscopic universe, as seen
by a huge giant. When you have written these pieces,
draw or paint these two opposing views of the world.
To start the project, write as many words as you can
think of that describe size and scale in the space below.

Project
The strong reflections of the rocks on the water make it look almost as if they are melting. Pick something solid –
a building, a car or a piece of furniture, for example. Draw it as it is, then do a series of drawings showing it
melting bit by bit, until it is completely liquid, reduced to a pool on the ground.

In the French Rooms, find:
Bords du Canal du Loing à St Mammès,
Alfred Sisley
(1839-1899)

This is a very different kind of scene, with water in it. Describe the differences between this painting and the last one:

O'Conor	Sisley

Sisley's brushstrokes vary quite a lot in this painting. Describe three different areas where his brushstrokes change. Describe the strokes. Sketch the direction of the brushstrokes.

Area			
Brushstrokes			
Sketch			

The first two landscapes depicted Holland and Ireland. This scene and the previous one are set in France, much further south. Do you notice any differences in the weather, in the landscape, or in the light?

Design project
Junior level: Design a T-shirt (front and back) based on one of these themes: under the sea, over the rainbow, *or* splash. *If you have silkscreens in your classroom you could print it.*
Senior level: Design a 2-page tourist brochure on transport, travel and tourism in this country.

Drawing Project
Draw a horizontal line halfway down a big page. Draw some interesting buildings along this line – castles, towers, skyscrapers, funfair rides. Imagine that they're at the edge of an island on a lake. Draw their reflections in the water beneath them, experimenting with different ways of drawing them so that they look as if they're on water.
When you've finished, try sticking cling-film over the reflections, to make them look even more like water.

Post-Primary Worksheet 6
Every Picture Tells a Story

National
Gallery *of*
IRELAND

In the Icon Room, find:
The Attempted Martyrdom of Saints Cosmas and Damian with their Brothers,
Fra Angelico (1387-1455)

Saints Cosmas and Damian were twins, both doctors who worked for free.
They were persecuted for refusing to pray to pagan statues, and managed to
survive attempts to drown, crucify and stone them to death. Eventually they
were beheaded. Here Fra Angelico has shown the attempt to burn them alive
by fire, but the flames have burst away from them, setting fire to the soldiers
instead.

Imagine yourself as a television reporter at the scene of their execution,
reporting on what has taken place. Tell the story in a television presenter's style in the space below.

> **Did you know?**
> This altar was commissioned by
> Cosimo de' Medici. Cosmas was
> his patron saint, not only because
> of his first name, but because the
> surname Medici means medic, or
> doctor, and Cosmas and Damian,
> as doctors, were the family's
> saints.

Fra Angelico has used vivid colours and strong movement to capture the sense of drama of this story.

Colour this drawing of the work as accurately as you can, using the same strong colours.

> **Meet the artist**
> *Fra Angelico* was a Dominican friar
> who painted only religious subjects.
> He was one of the finest painters of
> the Early Italian Renaissance.

> **Project**
> *Fra Angelico's work was painted on
> a wooden panel, covered in a
> smooth layer of gesso, a type of
> plaster of Paris. The artist painted
> in tempera, which is pure powdered
> colour mixed with egg yolk.
> For your tempera painting, first
> prepare a plaster layer on a board.
> Mix either ground coloured chalk or
> powder paints with egg yolk to make
> your tempera paint. Tempera dries
> quickly so you will have to work
> rapidly. Paint your picture, and see
> whether you prefer this medium to
> modern paints and paper.*

In the Italian Rooms, find:
The Taking of Christ,
Michelangelo Merisi da Caravaggio (1571-1610)

Caravaggio's *The Taking of Christ* shows the moment when Judas identifies and betrays Christ to the soldiers by kissing him. This was painted only 150 years after Fra Angelico's work, but you can see the huge difference between the two pictures, and the dramatically different way in which they tell their stories.
List some of the differences between the two paintings below.

_____
_____
_____
_____
_____
_____

Meet the artist
Caravaggio's paintings caused as much controversy as his behaviour – he was often involved in brawls. His paintings were in high demand, but he was often criticised for making religious scenes too realistic, e.g. look at the dirt under Judas' fingernails.

Whereas Fra Angelico concentrated on dramatic action, Caravaggio was more interested in telling the story through gesture and emotion. This is why he focuses on faces and hands, as these are the most expressive areas. Draw some of the faces and hands below, writing the emotions they express beside them.

Did you know?
Caravaggio painted straight onto the canvas without doing any preliminary studies. You can see where he changed his mind after painting Judas' ear – he painted over it, and moved it down an inch.

Did you know?
This painting was in the Irish Jesuit House in Dublin, unknown for 70 years, because it was thought to be by a different painter. It was rediscovered in 1990 and given on indefinite loan to the National Gallery.

Project
*Caravaggio and Fra Angelico painted in very different styles. You've already listed a lot of the differences, so keep those in mind. Do a new painting of both of these scenes, but pretend that Angelico is painting **The Taking of Christ,** and Caravaggio the **Attempted Martyrdom**. What would they have done differently? When you've finished, see which version of the scenes you prefer – you might have improved on the originals!*

In the Spanish Room, find:
St Francis Receiving the Stigmata,
El Greco (Domenikos Theotokopoulos) (1541-1614)

There is also a story behind El Greco's *St Francis Receiving the Stigmata.* St Francis was on retreat on a mountain when he saw a vision – represented in the painting by an outline of a crucifix in the top left-hand corner, surrounded by a bright light. When he saw the vision, his hands, feet and side began to bleed, like the five wounds of Christ. The saint died five years later.

This painting is in a different style to the previous works. Try to describe the main features of El Greco's style:

_____

_____

_____

_____

Describe the mood of this painting and what the painter has done to create this mood:

The skull is used as a symbol of death, representing our inevitable end and reminding us that life is short. Think of other symbols for death and draw them in the box opposite.

Think of symbols with happier meanings. Draw some in this box.

Imagine the scene of this painting with a happy symbol instead of a skull. Would this be enough to change the mood of the painting or would you have to change something else as well? If so, what?

Meet the artist
El Greco means The Greek. El Greco was born on Crete, in Greece, although he lived most of his life in Spain. One notable difference in his style was the way he elongated (stretched) his figures.

Symbols have been used to tell stories for hundreds of years – think of the children of Lir, turned into swans, or the poisoned apple in the story of Snow White. Can you think of any other stories with symbols?

Design Project
Junior level: Design a book cover on one of these themes: magic, inside the earth, fire, mystery.
Senior level: Start a project to produce an advertising campaign on these issues: murder, crime, drugs. *You could include some of your symbols in these projects.*

In the Irish Rooms, find:
The Opening of the Sixth Seal,
Francis Danby (1793-1861)

Did you notice?
Some people are holding pearls and gold – the message being conveyed is that you can't take the things of this world into the next life.

What is the first thing you notice when you look at Danby's *The Opening of the Sixth Seal*?
Why do you think you noticed this first?
What is the next thing you notice?
Why?
Where does your eye move next on the canvas?
Why?
Danby has used all these details to direct your eye around the painting in order to tell you the story. Do you think this method works?

Why do you think he wants you to notice things in this order?

The subject of this picture is from the Book of Revelations in the Old Testament, which vividly describes the day of judgement at the end of the world. As the Sixth Seal is opened, the moon turns red, the ground opens, and volcanoes erupt. This is the main story in the painting, but if you look at the people in the bottom half, there are other, smaller stories taking place.
Draw any of the stories you can see in this box.

Subject link: English
Write a short story beginning 'It was the day the world would end...'

Did you notice?
The section of the canvas showing the slave being freed was cut out by a visitor when it was first exhibited, because slavery was a controversial subject at that time. Luckily the piece was found and replaced, but you can still see the marks on the canvas.

Do you think Danby was more interested in the people or in the overall scene?
Why?
Do you think El Greco was more interested in the scene or the saint?
Why?

Does this picture show the real end of the world? What do you think?

The world might end differently – what about asteroids hitting the planet, nuclear explosions, attacks from Mars, or other disasters?

Invent your own 'end of the world' story when you get back to your artroom. Paint your version of the scene on a large page – make it as dramatic as possible.

Meet the artist
Francis Danby was Irish but lived in England for most of his life. His dramatic paintings were very popular in his time.

Post-Primary Worksheet 7
Weird and Wonderful Wildlife

G N I

National Gallery of IRELAND

In the French Rooms, find:
A Group of Dead Game,
Alexandre-François Desportes (1661-1743)

> **Meet the artist**
> *Desportes* was the leading animal and still-life painter of his day. His patrons – those who bought his paintings – included King Louis XIV and Louis XV of France. Hunting was a popular pastime of the French nobility.

Can you imagine paintings like this one becoming popular again today? Why/Why not?

Do you think this painting would be suitable for use as a poster against bloodsports?

Draw more details, add text and/or colour to this line drawing to make more of an impact. Try to make a really powerful statement about the cruelty involved in bloodsports.

Take note of the difference in textures between the animals and the fruit. Which areas in the painting do these textures describe?

Soft	
Smooth	
Hard	
Rubbery	
Shiny	
Warm	
Cold	

Design a series of patterns in the boxes below using different textures from the painting, such as feathers, fur and leaves. When you get back to school, use these ideas as a basis for a repeat-pattern design. You could do a lino-print or a silkscreen print based on your design.

In the Irish Rooms, find:
Paroquets,
Edward Murphy
(*c.* 1796-1841)

There is a huge contrast between the wildlife in this painting and in the last one. Write a list of words in the box to describe the different groups of wildlife.

Group of Dead Game	Paroquets

These creatures also live in very different environments. Do you think both artists have shown their real habitats? Why / why not?

Draw a wilder environment for these exotic birds in the box below. Make it really different.

The colours in the two paintings are also very different – they create different feelings in each painting.
Describe the range of colours used in each, and the emotions suggested by them:

	Colour	**Emotion**
Desportes		
Murphy		

Meet the artist
Little is known about *Edward Murphy*, an Irish artist, who painted scenes with animals. He may have been influenced by 17th-century Dutch animal paintings.

In the Spanish Rooms, find:
St Jerome translating the Bible,
Nicolás Francés (c. 1400-1468)

What differences in technique can you see between oil painting (the last two paintings) and tempera (this and the next painting)?

Oil Painting	Tempera

Do the monks in the painting seem afraid of the lion? Why/why not?

The reason for including the lion in St Jerome's study refers back to an old legend about the saint. While he was living in Bethlehem, a limping lion appeared and frightened his monks away. St Jerome remained calm, and investigated the lion's paw, removing a thorn which was causing the lion to limp. The lion was so grateful that he became the saint's constant companion.
In this painting the saint is busy transcribing the Bible, so one of his monks is shown removing the thorn from the lion's paw.

This painting is very brightly coloured, almost like the colours in the pages of illuminated manuscripts, like the Book of Kells. In fact, this artist also practised manuscript painting.

Do a rough design for a manuscript page showing St Jerome extracting the thorn from the lion – use the box below to sketch your idea.
On your return to school you could develop this idea into a full-page drawing, in colour, using decorative patterns like those in the Book of Kells.

In the Icon Room, find:
The Miracle of St George and the Dragon,
Novgorod School (Early 15th century)

The animals in this painting are used as symbols. Does the dragon symbolise good or evil?
Why do you think so?

Which of the two do you think the horse symbolises?
Why?

What do these symbols tell you about the moral of this story?

This is an 'icon painting'. The Greek word *icon* means 'an image'. Icons are religious images usually illustrating Christ, the Holy Family and the saints.

All the paintings in this room in the Gallery are icons. Do you notice any unusual colour in the icons that you don't see in most pictures?
Are there any other features of icon paintings that make them different to other works? Look around the room and make a list in the box below.

Icons:

Project
Did you notice that when animals and people are together in a painting, the humans are usually in control? Rearrange 'St Jerome translating the Bible' and 'The Miracle of St George and the Dragon' so that this time the animals are in charge.

The artist has painted the animals in a very stylised way – he hasn't tried to make them look real.

Pick out some particularly stylised details of the animals and draw them in the box above.

Meet the artist:
'The Novgorod School' means that the artist(s) who painted this icon has not been identified, but came from Novgorod, in North Russia, where the icon was painted.

Did you know?
St George is often depicted killing a dragon, which is said to represent paganism and magical powers.

Did you notice?
There is a half-length figure of St Nicholas on the top left-hand corner of the painting, as well as the hand of God in the top right corner.

Design projects
Junior level: Draw an imaginative composition on the theme of Irish wildlife and their habitats. You could do it in cartoon form or based on real life.
Senior level: Design a poster for a campaign against cruelty to animals.

Post-Primary Worksheet 8
Music and Dance

National
Gallery *of*
IRELAND

In French Room No. 10, find:
Dancers in the Dressing Room,
Edgar Degas (1834-1917)

Do you think Degas has captured the backstage atmosphere in this picture? What kind of atmosphere is this?

Meet the artist
Edgar Degas was a French Impressionist painter who concentrated mainly on depicting people, rather than landscapes.

In this picture, Degas has shown the differences between the solid, heavy shapes and objects around the dancers, and their softness and lightness. Draw one light and one heavy area from the scene in the box opposite, and try to make them look exactly like they do in Degas' version.

Heavy	Light

The dancers are shown at rest backstage. Imagine the difference in their expression and pose once they go on-stage to dance. Do a very rough, loose sketch of the two dancers in motion, in this box, trying to get a sense of their movement rather than any details.

Project
Take an old notebook or small copybook and draw one of the ballerinas from this picture in simple lines on the outside edge of the first page. Draw her again and again on the next pages, moving her arms, legs and head very slightly each time. When you've finished drawing, flip the pages very quickly and watch the movement of the dancer.

Did you know?
This work is in pastel (a form of chalk), which was a medium favoured by Degas. He was a draughtsman, painter, printer, and, in later life, a sculptor.

Again in Room No. 10, find:
Pierrot,
Juan Gris (1887-1927)

This is a different type of painting to Degas' Ballet Dancers. Degas looks at light, shade and colour backstage, whereas Gris is looking at flat shapes and patterns.

Do you get a sense of music, dance or movement from this painting? If so, where? If not, why not?

Gris has created a scene that looks more like a still life than a person beside a table. How does he create this effect?

He uses almost a code to represent different objects – a clarinet, a violin and a newspaper. Draw his shorthand code for these objects in the boxes below.

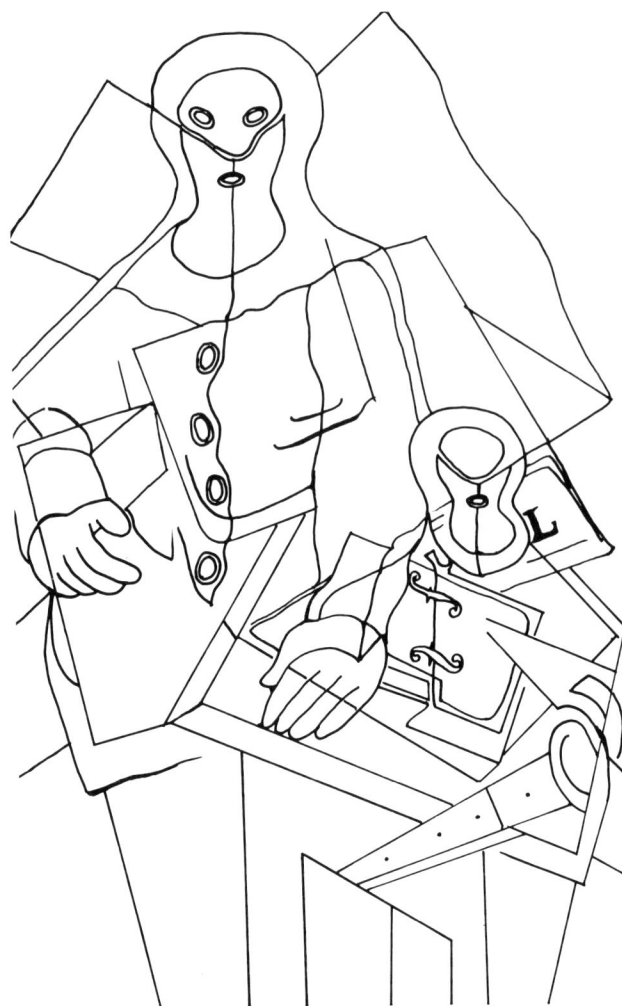

Violin	Newspaper	Clarinet

Use a similar code to represent the people and objects from the last painting by Degas. Using the line drawing on the last page as reference, draw a coded version of that painting in the box opposite.

Do you get the same sense of movement and dance from the coded version, or has it become more still?

Do you think this helps explain the difference between the works of these two artists?

Finally, colour and shade the line-drawing of the Pierrot above to change the objects from flat shapes to three-dimensional ones.
Does this make a difference to the painting? Why / why not?

Meet the artist
Juan Gris was a Spanish painter who learned about Cubism from Picasso. Cubism was a way of painting everyday things as very simple shapes, giving the impression of seeing the objects from several angles at once. Gris also designed costumes, illustrated books and painted portraits.

Did you notice?
Gris has put a glass on the table, which looks like a smaller version of the Pierrot's head. This might be to suggest that the Pierrot is a magician and that a performer or artist can make ordinary things magical.

In the Print Gallery, find:
Under the Big Top at a Circus,
Mainie Jellett (1897-1944)

The last painting, by Gris, was quite still, with little or no sense of movement or noise. Describe the effect of Jellett's painting:

How has she created this effect?

What are the main sounds, smells, sights, colours and textures you associate with the circus? Write or draw a few of them in the box opposite.

Meet the artist
Mainie Jellett is considered the leader of the modern movement in Ireland, and was one of the founders of the Irish Exhibition of Living Art. Her painting style was based on cubist principles.

Subject link: English
Write a poem or a piece of prose based on the circus. Think of some descriptive phrases you might use and write them here.

Illustrate the border of your poem, or passage, with symbols or details of the circus. Try out a few ideas in the box opposite.

The colours in this watercolour are much brighter than Gris' work. In fact, Jellett uses all the colours of the rainbow in this work. She uses cold colours – green, blue and purple – for the top half of the scene, and warm reds, oranges and yellows for the foreground.

Design a new colour scheme for this picture, taking artificial lighting in the tent into account. You could add big coloured spotlights and modern lighting effects to the scene to make it more interesting.

Project
Produce life-sized drawings for a series of costumes, for men and women, for one of the following acts: jockeys, clowns, acrobats, animal trainers, ring-master/mistress.
You could make your costumes realistic, or totally outrageous.

In the Dutch Rooms, find:
The Lute Player,
Studio of Frans Hals (*c.* 1580/3-1666)

Do you get a feeling of music being played in this picture? Explain:

Hals decided not to paint a background for *The Lute Player* because he wanted the viewer to concentrate on the figure. This leaves us free to imagine the rest of the scene – is he playing for himself, or for people dancing, or for people listening? Which do you think?

Draw a background for this picture.

The lute player's gaze seems to follow you as you move around the room. What kind of man do you think this lute player might have been? What kind of music do you think he would have liked to play?

Imagine a musical nightmare – a combination of the four pictures, with the lute player and the pierrot playing their instruments at the circus, and the ballet dancers in the circus ring with the riders.

Draw a suitably lively version of this scene in the box opposite. You could show the reaction of the crowd too.

Post-Primary Worksheet 9
Town and Country

National Gallery of IRELAND

In the Dutch Rooms, find:
Lady Writing a Letter, with her Maid,
Johannes Vermeer (1632-75)

Do you think the women in the painting look as if they are posing, or do they seem unaware of the artist's presence? Explain your answer:

> **Did you know?**
> In 17th-century Dutch painting, letter-writing was a popular subject and traditionally it related to the theme of love.

In the box below, use your imagination to draw the view which the maid could be looking at from the window in this painting. Is it a town or a country scene? Remember that this painting is set in Holland!

> **Project**
> *Examine the shapes and colours of the stained-glass window in this painting. Design your own stained-glass window. To do this draw and cut out a stencil from thick black paper, then place this stencil on top of a sheet of white paper of the same size. This will give the effect of a leaded window. You can then paint the different sections in different colours.*

Meet the artist
Johannes Vermeer was a Dutch artist who painted mostly genre scenes (everyday scenes) like this one. He painted very slowly, concentrating on detail. Just over thirty of his paintings survive.

Project
Vermeer often uses a large black-and-white tiled background. Try designing your own tiled floor. Examine the patterned tiling in this Gallery in rooms 9 and 14. When you get home, design your own floor pattern.

In the Dutch Rooms, find:
A Wooded Landscape – the Path on the Dyke,
Meindert Hobbema (1638-1709)

This scene depicted here is typical of the Dutch countryside. If you look closely to the left of this work, you can see a tiny church steeple and a windmill. Draw enlarged versions of these two buildings in the box below.

The people in this painting clearly have a very different life to those in the previous one.

Fill in the two cartoon strips below with humorous scenes, one showing a day in the life in the Dutch countryside, the other a day in the life in a Dutch city. Don't forget to include speech bubbles.

In the country...			
In the town...			

The figures and the animals in this painting were not actually painted by Hobbema but by another artist named Adrian Van de Velde. Describe the differences between these two artists' styles:

Junior level project
Hobbema would have made a number of outdoor studies before he did this painting. Here is a simple variation on outdoor studies. Take a piece of paper and hold it against a textured object, for example the bark of a tree, then rub the paper with a crayon. You can do this with any number of other items as well: leaves, car tyres, walls etc. You could include these rubbings in a larger work, for example a landscape or a still life with foliage.

In Room 12, find:
The Gleaners,
Jules Breton (1827-1906)

There is a clue in this work that this scene is set in France. Draw it in the box below.

Does this scene look like the weather and scenery you would expect to see in France?
Describe the differences between French weather and scenery, and that in Holland (as seen in the previous painting).

The colours in this painting are different to those in the last one, possibly because of the difference in weather. What vivid colours has the artist used to bring the picture to life?

How do the shapes of haystacks in France compare to those in Ireland?

Draw Irish and French haystacks side by side in the box opposite. Which shape do you prefer?

Do the people in this painting look like very poor people? Why / why not?

Many of the peasants are barefoot, but some are wearing clogs. Design a modern pair of clogs in this box, and decorate them using bright colours.

In the Irish Rooms, find:
St. Patrick's Close, Dublin,
Walter Osborne (1859-1903)

Meet the artist
Walter Osborne, an Irish artist who studied in Holland and France, often painted everyday scenes of Dublin. He didn't prettify the scenes – he always painted what he saw.
Look at the way in which he has painted the people, the buildings and the street.

Imagine if the sun could shine through the smoggy atmosphere in Osborne's cityscape, and how it would change the colours and the shadows in the scene. On the drawing below, colour and shade the scene as if it were bright sunlight. You could use some of Breton's bright colours from the previous painting.

Do you see any similarities in the lives of the different people in all the paintings on this worksheet?

This painting suggests experiences for many of the 5 senses.
Do you think this is a noisy or a quiet picture?

Does it suggest any smells to you?

What would the different surfaces feel like to touch?

Dublin in the 1880s would have been quite different to the French countryside in the 1850s. Describe the different sounds, smells and textures in the two pictures. Be as descriptive as you can – pretend you are describing it over the phone to someone in another country. Write your descriptions in the box below.

Do you think that the young boy at the front of the painting is playing a happy or a sad tune on his whistle? Why?

Design projects
Junior level: Design a poster to promote your city, town or county.
Senior level: Design a leaflet to educate people about the following: poverty, homelessness, *and* rural and urban unemployment.

Subject link: History
Write a short essay called 'A Day in Four Lives', describing a day in the life of one person from each painting. Try to give as much historical background as you can.

© Gailearaí Náisiúnta na hÉireann, Education Department, Merrion Square West, Dublin 2 · Phone 01-661 5133 · Fax 01-676 6488

Post-Primary Worksheet 10
Signs and Symbols

National
Gallery of
IRELAND

In the Irish Rooms, find:
The Conjuror,
Nathaniel Hone the Elder
(1718-1784)

In this scene a magician is waving his wand to conjure up prints and paintings by famous artists from a fire.

But there is more to this picture than meets the eye. The painting is about one artist attacking another, accusing him of conjuring up paintings by imitating older works. The artist uses symbols to show this.

Meet the artist
Nathaniel Hone, an Irish artist who lived and worked in London, initially painted portrait miniatures, before turning to portrait and subject pictures. He was influenced by Dutch painting. The artist he attacked in this picture, Joshua Reynolds, was a follower of Italian art, which was in a very different style. Reynolds was also the president of the Royal Academy, the main art institution in England. Was Hone wise to attack him?

Look at *The Earl of Bellamont*, painted in the Italian grand manner by Joshua Reynolds, in the English Rooms. Which painting style do you prefer – the one used by Reynolds or Hone? Why?

Draw and colour the following symbols on the line drawing above. Hone used each one to attack Reynolds.

Owl	Symbol of wisdom in Italian art, but meant folly or stupidity in Dutch painting.
Star of David	Used to be associated with magic.
Face of the conjuror	Hone persuaded George White, Reynolds' favourite model, to pose for this scene.
Cascading prints	Reynolds copied poses from many of these Italian paintings by Raphael, Michelangelo, etc.

Did you notice?
The devil can be seen flying off through the second window. Hone may be suggesting that he is supplying the prints for Reynolds' inspiration.

Did you know?
In the window at the top left corner of the painting, Hone originally painted seven nudes, including one of an artist friend of Reynolds', Angelica Kauffmann. She refused to let the picture be exhibited until Hone painted her out, so he replaced it with this scene showing Reynolds and his friends around a table. The original version can still be seen by x-ray.

In the Italian Rooms, find:
Spring and Summer,
Bernardo Strozzi
(1581-1644)

What symbols has Strozzi surrounded these two figures with: Spring (on the right) and Summer (on the left)? Draw, colour and explain them below.

Explanation:			

Invent, draw and explain your own symbols representing Spring and Summer – try not to use fruit or flowers.

Explanation:			

Strozzi has used different colours for Spring and Summer. Make a chart of Spring and Summer colours, based on the painting, and design your own charts for Autumn and Winter.

Spring   Summer   Autumn   Winter

In the Dutch Rooms, find:
A Vanitas Fruit Piece,
Jan Davidsz. de Heem
(1606-1683)

The symbols in this painting are all reminders that life on earth is short, but that there is life after death.

What symbols of death can you see?

There are also symbols of life after death. Corn is one of these – it has to be buried in order to grow. Can you see any others (look closely around the bunches of green grapes)?

What two things can you see on the table in the bottom left-hand corner?

What is this particular food and drink a symbol of (think of the overall theme of the painting)?

The snake is also important as a reference to the fall of Adam and Eve from the Garden of Eden, as the start of the journey through life.

Did you think that this was a religious picture when you first looked at it? Why?

Do you think it is now? Why?

Do you think it would be as interesting if it was a simple still life, without these other symbols and meanings?

The fruit and colours in this painting look as if they belong in late Summer. Go back to the season colour charts you drew for the last painting. Pick a different season to colour this illustration, and see if it changes the effect.

Meet the artist
Jan de Heem was a well-known Dutch painter who specialised in still-life scenes in the 17th century.

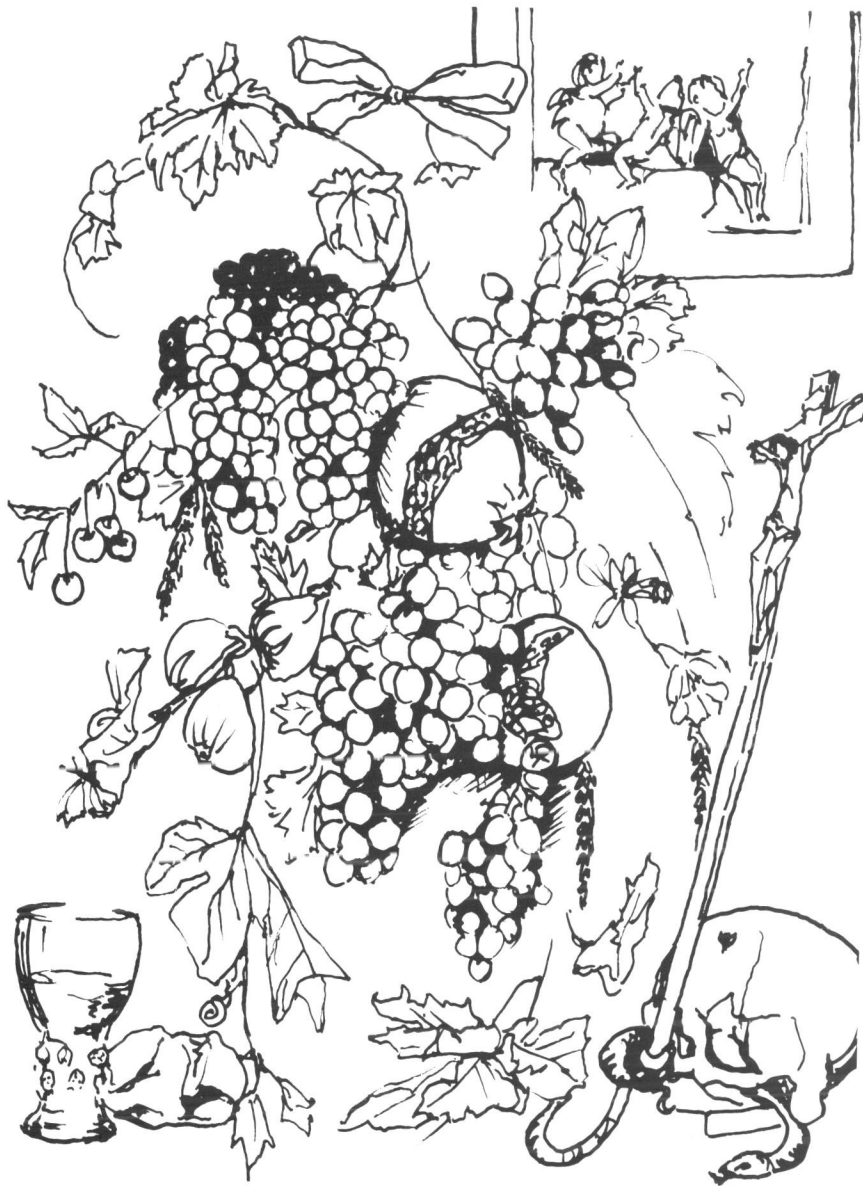

Did you know?
Vanitas is a Latin word which means 'empty' – in this picture it means the emptiness of worldly goods. The artist is emphasising spiritual life over material wealth.

Did you know?
The moral of this painting, which is that life on earth is short but there is a better life after death, is very similar to that in *The Opening of the Sixth Seal* by Francis Danby, in the Irish Rooms. This painting shows the end of the world, with people desperately clinging to their jewellery and valuables, while the only person left standing is the slave, who has been freed.
Look for this painting in the Gallery, and see which artist you think explains the theme more successfully.

In the Icon Room, find:
The Annunciation,
Jacques Yverni
(1410-1438)

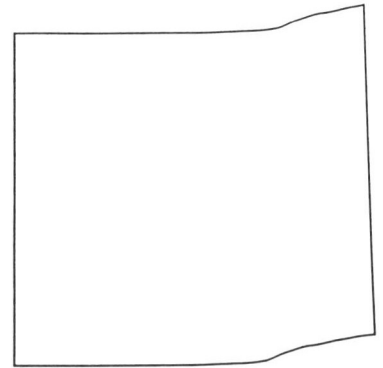

What is the story of the Annunciation?

Who does the dove represent in this painting (it is just above the lily)?

Can you guess who the red figure is, coming down to the Virgin Mary between God and the dove?
Draw it in as much detail as you can in the box above.

The Lily is a symbol of purity, relating to the figure of the Virgin Mary. What is it about this flower that symbolises purity, in your opinion?

The saint on the left is Stephen, the first Christian martyr. He was stoned to death. The palm leaf he is holding is a symbol of martyrdom. In the box opposite, draw the symbol Yverni used to show how the saint died.

The two small figures on the left represent the donor, who commissioned this painting, and her chaplain or priest. What makes these figures different from the other ones? (Look carefully)

Design projects
Junior level: Look at the colour and texture of the angel's wings. They look very different to the white shiny wings you see in a lot of paintings. Design and make a full-sized pair of wings for yourself. Think about what materials to use, their structure and texture, and the different patterns and colours you could paint onto them.
Senior level: Design a symbol or logo for Christmas or Easter, and use this in a poster to advertise a Church service.

Meet the artist
Jacques Yverni, a French artist, painted religious subjects, but only two of his paintings survived the bombing of France during World War II. One is in Dublin, the other in Italy.

Did you know?
Avignon, in France, where this was painted, became the residence of the Pope for over sixty years in the 14th century. That is the reason why so many religious paintings were produced there.

GENERAL IRISH ART

B. Arnold. *A Concise History of Irish Art.* Thames & Hudson, 1969

A. Crookshank and The Knight of Glin. *The Painters of Ireland 1660-1920.* Barrie & Jenkins, 1978

A. Crookshank and The Knight of Glin. *The Watercolours of Ireland.* Barrie & Jenkins, 1994

B. Fallon. *Irish Art 1830-1900.* Appletree Press, 1994

P. Harbison, H. Potterton & J. Sheehy. *Irish Art and Architecture.* Thames & Hudson, 1987

B. P. Kennedy. *Irish Painting.* Town House & Country House, 1993

B. P. Kennedy and R. Gillespie (Eds). *Ireland – Art into History.* Town House & Country House, 1994

S. B. Kennedy, *Irish Art and Modernism.* Institute of Irish Studies, 1991

P. Larmour. *The Arts and Crafts Movement.* Friars Bush Press, 1994

K. McConkey. *A Free Spirit Irish Art 1860-1960.* Antique Collectors Club & Pyms Gallery, 1990

W. Ryan Smolin, E. Mayes & J. Rogers (Eds). *Irish Women Artists,* National Gallery of Ireland, 1987

J. Sheehy. *The Rediscovery of Ireland's Past – The Celtic Revival 1830-1930.* Thames & Hudson, 1980

T. Snoddy. *A Dictionary of Irish Artists in the Twentieth Century.* Wolfhound Press, 1996

A. Stewart. Royal Hibernian Academy of Arts. *Index of Exhibitors 1826-1976.* Manton Publishing, Dublin. Vol 1 1985, Vol 2 1986, Vol 3 1987

W. Strickland. *A Dictionary of Irish Artists.* 2 Vols. 1913. Reprinted Irish Academic Press, 1989

D. Walker. *Modern Art in Ireland.* Lilliput Press, 1997

IRISH ARTISTS

B. Arnold. *Mainie Jellett and the Modern Movement in Ireland.* Yale University Press, 1991

B. Arnold. *Orpen: Mirror to an Age.* Jonathan Cape, 1981

R. Bennington. *Roderic O'Conor.* Irish Academic Press, 1992

M. Bourke. 'Frederic William Burton; Painter, Antiquarian and Art Historian', *Eire-Ireland. Journal of Irish Studies,* Minnesota, 1991

M. Bourke. 'Portrait of Evie Hone in her Studio by Hilda van Stockum', *Studies.* Summer 1997

J. Campbell. *The Irish Impressionists in Ireland, France and Belgium.* National Gallery of Ireland, 1984

J. Campbell. *Mary Swanzy.* Pyms Gallery, London, 1986

J. Campbell. *Frank O'Meara.* Hugh Lane Municipal Gallery of Modern Art, 1986

J. Campbell. *Nathaniel Hone the Younger.* National Gallery of Ireland, 1992

A. Crookshank. *Mildred Anne Butler.* Town House/National Gallery of Ireland, 1992

C. Crouan. *Maurice MacGonigal.* Hugh Lane Municipal Gallery of Modern Art, 1991

D. Ferran. *Leech: An Irish Painter Abroad.* National Gallery of Ireland, 1996

N. Gordon Bowe. *The Life and Work of Harry Clarke.* Irish Academic Press, 1989

N. Gordon Bowe, D. Caron & M. Wynne. *Gazetter of Irish Stained Glass 1903-63.* Dublin 1988

F. Greenacre. *Francis Danby.* Tate Gallery, London, 1988

J. Hutchinson. *James Arthur O'Connor.* National Gallery of Ireland, 1985

S. B. Kennedy. *Paul Henry.* Town House/National Gallery of Ireland, 1991

A. Le Harivel. *Nathaniel Hone the Elder.* Town House/National Gallery of Ireland, 1992

A. Le Harivel, *100 Years of Watercolours.* National Gallery of Ireland, 1997

K. McConkey. *Sir John Lavery.* Cannongate press, Edinburgh, 1993

A. Maher and C. de Courcy. *Fifty Views of Ireland.* National Gallery of Ireland, 1985

K. O'Brien. *Harry Kernoff RHA.* Martello, Spring 1990

A. O'Connor. 'James Latham: Two Portraits', *Burlington Magazine,* Vol 116, 1974

J. O'Grady. *The Life and Work of Sarah Purser.* Four Courts Press, 1996

R. Ormond and J. Turpin. *Daniel Maclise 1808-70.* Arts Council of Great Britain, 1972

M. Pointon. *Mulready.* Victoria and Albert Museum, London, 1986

W. L. Pressly. *The Life and Art of James Barry.* Yale University Press, 1981

H. Pyle. *Yeats: Portrait of an Artistic Family.* National Gallery of Ireland, 1997

H. Pyle. *Jack B. Yeats: a Biography.* London, 1970

RHA. *Sean Keating.* Royal Hibernian Academy, Dublin 1989

J. Sheehy. *Walter Osborne.* National Gallery of Ireland, 1983

J. White. *Gerard Dillon. An Illustrated Biography.* Wolfhound Press, 1994

M. Wynne. *Irish Stained Windows.* Easons, 1977

M. Wynne. 'Thomas Roberts 1748-78', *Studies,* 1977

M. Wynne. 'Thomas Rye', *Burlington Magazine,* London, Vol 124, 1982

M. Wynne. *Fifty Irish Painters.* National Gallery of Ireland, 1983

WRITING WORKSHEETS AND ACTIVITY SHEETS

Worksheets and activity sheets are one of the best ways of occupying young people in a museum or gallery. It would be a mistake, however, to view them merely as time-fillers because they also perform a useful learning function. By focusing attention on works of art, they help young people to appreciate and understand them better. They also encourage students to explore the context in which works of art were created, and often they give them greater confidence in learning new ideas. Teachers feel comfortable with worksheets and themesheets because they enable students rapidly to come to terms with aspects of the Collection at a point when they are planning a visit to the Gallery. While the worksheets are normally provided in the Gallery, Transition Year teachers distribute them back in the classroom as a way of consolidating information and reinforcing the visit. If parents, teachers and young people benefit from and enjoy using worksheets, then it is worth spending the time finding out how to make them practical and effective. These guidelines may help and encourage you to write your own worksheets and activity sheets.

Steps for organising/writing worksheets and activity sheets

1. **Write the worksheet or activity sheet for a specific age-group**, e.g. tiny tots (age 3-5), children (age 6-12), teenagers (age 13-18) and adults. Puzzle and clue sheets can be aimed at the 12-15 age-group. Make it effective by gradually progressing from the simple to the complex. Define difficult terms, keep sentences short, words simple, and give clear instructions.

2. **Vary the questions** by first asking ones that require easy answers (yes/no, how many?, what?, which?). Follow this with questions that require some thought (how do x and y differ?, imagine that you…, describe…, is x significant?). Progress to questions that need a view or an opinion (do you agree?, what do you think?, how could x be important?).

3. **Design attractive and well-laid-out worksheets and activity sheets.** Divide the sheet into different areas, e.g. questions, information, drawings and projects. It helps to vary the size of the typeface – use bold lettering, italics and capitals. Label clearly, and use small boxes for 'either/or' questions, for highlighting specific points, e.g. 'Did you notice?', 'Meet the artist', 'Did you know?', 'Subject links'. It is of great help if the various boxes can be shaded so that they stand out on the page. Provide variety through exercises, e.g. word searches, crosswords, treasure trails, spotting similarities, joining matching pairs, quizzes, etc.

4. **Good illustrations are essential.** Illustrations must be of the highest standard possible. Good worksheets and activity sheets vary the nature of the illustrations, employing photographs, maps, line-drawings, painted images and cartoons. Use your computer to create the artwork and print the worksheet.

5. **Include projects.** Every worksheet and activity sheet should include a project, regardless of whether it is aimed at tiny tots, children, teenagers or even adults. The purpose of the project is to encourage the participant to engage in another related activity once the worksheet is completed. The projects can range from something easy to

something quite difficult. Aim the project at a specific age-group and make this obvious, e.g. 'Tiny Tots' Project and make this obvious, e.g. 'Lower Primary Project', or 'Little People's Project', Project'. For teenagers: 'Junior Cycle Project', 'Transition Year Project' and 'Senior Primary Project'. Use simple language to describe the project and make the description clear and brief.

6. **Relate the worksheet to the curriculum.** If you want students to use worksheets, then spend time doing research, asking the advice of other teachers and relating the worksheets to their work/study programme. The curriculum positively encourages the use of this type of resource and museums and galleries provide many opportunities to develop them further.

MAKING WORKSHEETS AND ACTIVITY SHEETS LOOK EASY

Before you begin to write a worksheet, develop a themesheet or design an activity sheet, and make sure you have your research information and illustrations to hand. For children with different learning abilities or special needs, the worksheet or activity sheet should be *short, well designed*, with *simple vocabulary*, and adaptable to include *structured activities*.

A different approach, and one that is more allied with the art curriculum, is to write a *worksheet based on themes*, including portraits, landscapes, narratives, history painting, religious painting or still-life, all of which are included in the book **Exploring Art at the National Gallery**. The new series of themed worksheets for post-primary students, included in this book, is also available by writing to the Gallery's Education Department.

There is another set of *project-based activity sheets* available from the Education Department, entitled the **EyeSpy Series**, which include the following:

* Tiny Tots' EyeSpy Activity Sheet
* Children's EyeSpy Activity Sheet
* Teenagers' EyeSpy Activity Sheet
* Adult EyeSpy
* EyeSpy Picture Puzzles

Puzzle activity sheets, which contain hints and clues, cartoons and half-completed drawings, poems and funny questions, are popular because they are

unpredictable and require that the student approach the works of art in a different way. They can be both fun and frustrating for the student, who, nonetheless, feels a great sense of achievement when the puzzles have been solved.

Another idea is to provide your students with an *unusual situation*, for example, suggest that they are film producers looking for a location to shoot a thriller. It is a complex film because it involves detectives, the police, the victim, and the murderer. Suggest that they investigate the National Gallery as a possible location for the film. Instruct the students to sketch the layout of the rooms, noting the position of the pictures, sculptures, display cases and furniture. Mark in the windows, doors and stairs, taking into account lighting and sound requirements. Plan the film sets taking note of the location, furniture, equipment and special-effects required. Notes on hair, make-up, costumes and lighting will also be important. The students should finalise the project by presenting a film schedule in the form of a pro-posal, with a number of story-boards depicting the scenes as the story unfolds.

This type of situation, where students can project themselves into the role of someone like a film pro-ducer, newspaper reporter or TV presenter, is ideal because it allows them the opportunity to *use their imaginations* and *give free expression to their ideas*. It also requires that they view the works of art and Gallery rooms from a very different perspective. This can produce some very interesting results, plus a feel-ing of great satisfaction when the project is completed.

These suggestions represent a number of different approaches to worksheets, theme sheets and activity sheets. When your first worksheet or activity sheet has been drafted, test it out on a number of adults, teenagers, and children of different ages. Use a sim-ple method to evaluate it – either it is effective or it isn't! Don't be too discouraged if it was not a great success – just review the design, clarify the questions, reduce and simplify the text and try it out again. Comfort yourself in the knowledge that the perfect worksheet or activity sheet has not yet been written!

SETTING UP A CLASSROOM MUSEUM & EXHIBITION

This chapter gives step-by-step instructions on how Transition Year students can set up a classroom museum and mount an exhibition.

CREATING A CLASSROOM MUSEUM

Transition Year students have a unique opportunity to combine their skills to create a classroom museum. In the process of making their own museum, students will be able to sharpen their research, data-gathering, organisational and problem-solving skills, while experiencing the excitement of learning about the past through clues found close to home.

There are museums and galleries in most of the world's major towns and cities. Before the students set about creating their own classroom museum, you might suggest that they visit a local museum or his-toric site, paying particular attention to its content, layout and design. Encourage the students on their return to describe the museum, gallery or stately house they visited and ask them to draw the design and layout of the building, noting entrances and exits, windows and lighting, and any unusual features. Give them some time to think about and analyse the museum. Once all these matters have been discussed, the students will be ready to embark upon their project.

There are three elements involved in making a museum:

* selecting a subject;
* collecting objects and information relating to the subject;
* deciding how the objects will be arranged and displayed.

Classroom museum floor-plan (B. Drinan)

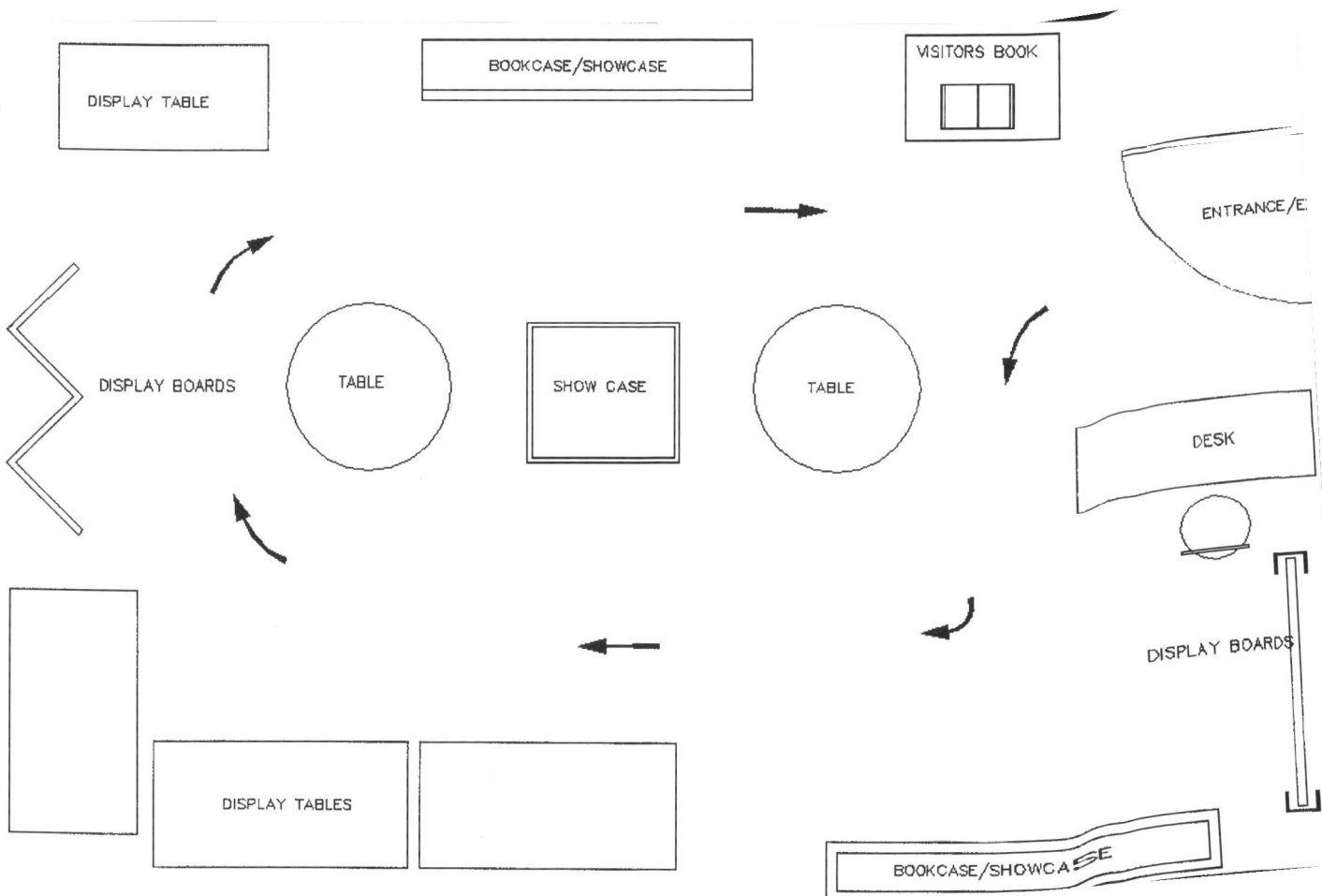

The following steps should be followed by the students, under the teacher's guidance.

1. Choose a theme, such as 'School Sporting Achievements', 'School Personalities' or 'The History of the School'.

2. Plan how to go about collecting the objects and information needed for the display. This is the most difficult task. It might be a good idea to divide the young people into small groups and allocate a different activity to each group. The following are examples of the types of activities the students themselves might undertake in small groups for a theme such as 'The History of the School':

* Set up interviews with past and present principals, the architect, board members, donors, past and present teachers and pupils.
* Visit local resource centres for gathering information, e.g. the library, newspapers, a museum or gallery, town hall and planning office, the local heritage centre.
* Search out photographs of the school in its early years by contacting past pupils. Include building plans and architects' drawings.
* Advertise for other memorabilia: school reports, letters, textbooks, class projects, trophies, sports equipment and pictures.
* Hunt out old desks, chairs, blackboards, science equipment, cameras, sewing machines, maps, charts, etc to put in the museum.
* Consider seeking donations from past pupils and the local community.

3. Ask the principal for a spare room in which to house the museum.

4. Decide how the objects will be arranged and displayed on panels, tables and bookcases. Install and clearly label the exhibits, noting the name and date of the object, when it was acquired and why it is important.

5. Assign a number of students to list all the exhibits and to write a brief guide to the museum.

6. Appoint a team of students to look after publicity. This will involve making posters, typing up

invitations for the official opening and writing a press release. They should advertise the posters locally, send out the invitations and contact the newspapers about the museum opening. Invite past and present pupils, teachers, parents and members of the local community to the opening reception.

7. Plan the opening day, requesting the principal to launch the museum.

8. Organise the class on a rota basis so that there are students available to explain and interpret the museum and exhibits to the visitors. Encourage everyone to visit the museum and enjoy the displays.

9. After the opening, have a party for all those who contributed to the project.

A further suggestion: Transition Year students might also be interested in creating a local history museum. Local history is the history of a street e.g. Wexford Street, a neighbourhood – Sandymount, a city – Cork, a town – Clifden, a village – Ballyvaughan, a county – Donegal, or even a large area such as the province of Ulster, or a region such as The Midlands. Once everyone knows what a local history museum is, arrange to visit one so that the students can see for themselves how objects are displayed and interpreted for visitors.

ORGANISING AN EXHIBITION

No matter where Transition Year students live, or what type of community they come from, they can benefit from drawing on materials found in their own school, neighbourhood and local community to create their own exhibition. Besides gaining experience in research, hanging and mounting, writing and problem-solving, they will learn a great deal about their community, as well as the fundamentals of exhibition design.

You will need to allow plenty of time to plan the exhibition. You might suggest to the students that they visit different exhibitions, so that they can discuss details of the layout and display before they begin work on their own. Get them to record their findings, e.g. notes and drawings, in a folder and to use this for reference purposes. Many museums and galleries mount special temporary exhibitions, so there should be a number of options for students to research. To be suitable, the exhibition room must have public access, sufficient hanging space, good lighting, some form of control of the heating and humidity levels, and it must be safe and secure. The principal might give permission to book the local community hall and the students could paint the walls a neutral colour for the exhibition.

There are three key elements to an exhibition:

* selecting a theme;

* acquiring objects and information relating to the theme;

* deciding how the objects will be mounted and displayed.

The following steps should be taken:

1. Try to select a popular subject like 'Art and the Environment', 'Peace and Violence' or 'Wildlife'.

2. The students need a plan to help them go about securing works for the exhibition. Form them into small groups and assign each group a separate task. For example:

* Type up a notice outlining exhibition entry details: the name and address of the artist; the number and title of the sculptures, paintings, objects or photographs being submitted (mounted and framed); the size and medium of the items. Specify the entry date.

* Put notices advertising the exhibition in the library, town hall, shops, schools, church and community hall.

* Seek a local business, preferably one relevant to the subject, to finance the venture.

* Appoint a team of students to select the works to be exhibited, to plan the display, to install the exhibits, and to write and attach a label to each one. It is important that the labels are large enough to be read comfortably. Exhibits can be mounted on display-board panels or set out on tables and bookcases. Decide if the pictures will be hung along the line of the top, middle or bottom of the frame, and make sure they are hung at a level that allows for easy viewing. Allocate appropriate space to each work of art. Check that the lighting is of sufficient strength for the display to be seen clearly, and that it does not cause any damage to the works of art.

* A student who is good at writing could look after the catalogue. Each entry should contain the artist's name, the name of the lender, the title of the work, the measurements and medium, e.g. oil, watercolour, bronze or wood. The principal could write the introduction, thanking the sponsor and exhibitors, while the art teacher could write a few paragraphs on the theme. Nominate a student to photograph exhibits for the catalogue cover and for the press. The catalogue could be printed on the school computer and the class could help with folding and stapling.

3. Display a check-list chart outlining dates and deadlines leading up to the opening.

4. Invite a prominent figure, perhaps the mayor, a wildlife or environmental personality if the subject is 'Wildlife', or the sponsor, to open the exhibition.

5. Assign several students to look after the invitations and reception. Make sure the artists, business people, local community groups, teachers, parents and students all receive invitations.

6. Phone the newspapers and radio and television stations. Have catalogues, press releases and photographs ready so that the press can view the exhibition before the launch.

7. Work out a timetable so that each student takes a turn looking after the exhibits and selling catalogues.

8. Assign one student to record the event on video for the school archives.

9. To help create awareness of the exhibition, organise support activities, including talks for adults, tours of the display, and workshops for children. Invite family, friends, neighbours and relatives and enjoy guiding them around the exhibition.

10. Prior to the opening, have a party for everyone involved in the project.

A further suggestion: Devise an exhibition to show the transformation in Irish life and culture from the first millennium to the second millennium. Make projections for the future. Define what you mean by 'culture'. How will students describe and illustrate the social and political background to the period, together with aspects of the heritage? What significance will the exhibition have for the audience and the many artists e.g. painters, writers, musicians? Consider the type of materials to be gathered and discuss how they will be displayed and interpreted. This suggestion could form the basis of a major project for students in Transition Year.

Exhibition Hall floor-plan (B. Drinan)

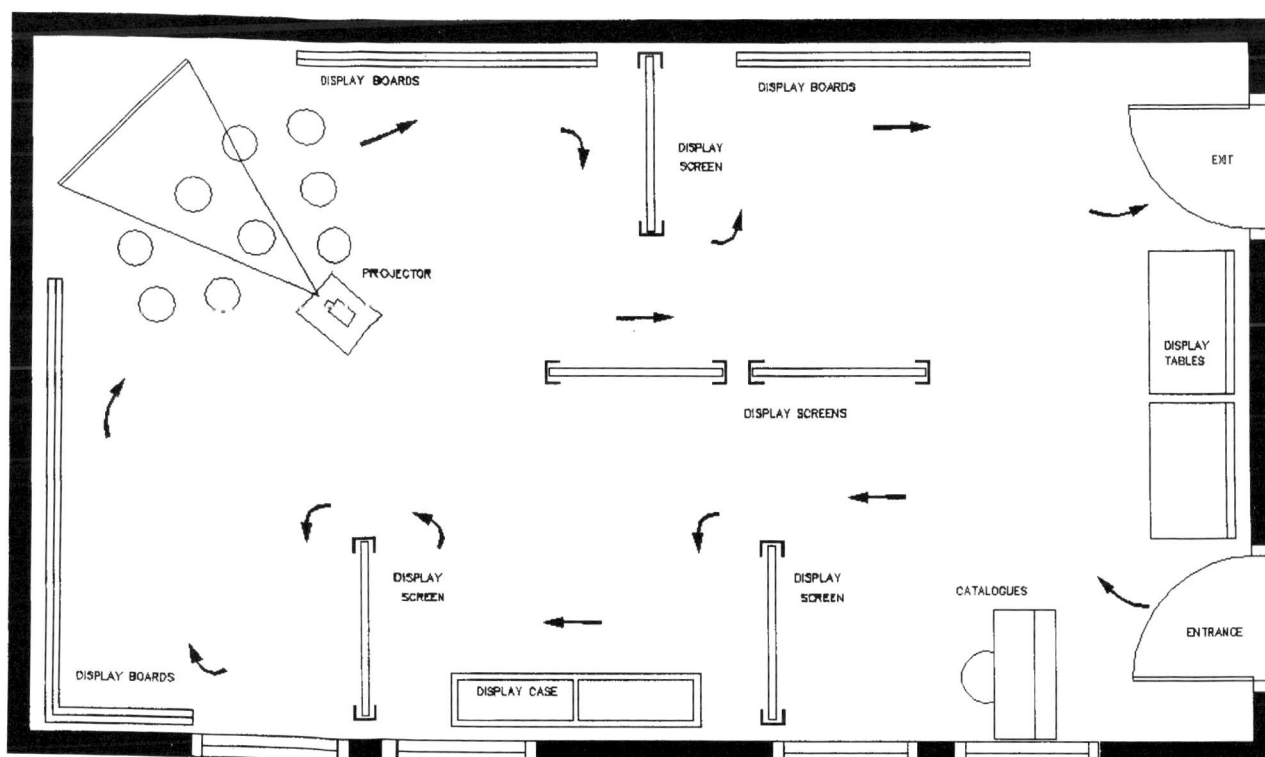

SOME FACTS ABOUT THE NATIONAL GALLERY OF IRELAND

* The paintings in the National Gallery belong to the Irish nation – everyone is welcome to visit and view them. Each year the Gallery has over one million visitors.

* Admission to the Gallery is free.

* Opening hours are: Monday to Saturday 10am – 5.30pm, Thursday 11am – 8.30pm, Sunday 2pm – 5pm. The Gallery is closed on Good Friday, and 24, 25 and 26 December.

* The National Gallery seeks to provide a service that is equally accessible to all its visitors. Details of its programmes and activities are published quarterly in *Gallery News*, which is available free of charge from the Information Desk.

* Visitor aids include an information service, guide-books, floor-plans, multimedia and audio guides.

* The National Gallery encourages families to visit, by putting on a Family Programme and special events for teenagers, children and tiny tots.

* Ramps, lifts, wheelchairs, induction loops, toilets, phones and other facilities are provided for people with disabilities and special needs. There are Braille guides and also tours using Tactile Picture Sets for people with impaired sight, and tours with an interpreter for people with impaired hearing. The Gallery's *Access Guide* highlights these events.

* The Gallery Shop and Restaurant, located on the ground floor, are open during Gallery hours.

* The National Gallery of Ireland's comprehensive Education Service includes:

The Public Programme: Public lectures and tours, tours for people with special needs, and the Family Programme.

Continuing Education: Drawing and Art Appreciation courses for adults.

Young People's Activities: The Schools Programme comprising: art lectures, portfolio days, Transition Year Option, study revision days, school tours and a wide range of worksheets. Other events include: teenagers' drawing course, children's summer club, little masters' drawing classes and the Christmas art holiday. Children's art exhibitions are held on occasion.

Community Awareness and Outreach Programme: This includes the disability service and the annual Family Day. The Outreach Programme brings the Gallery to a wider public throughout the country by means of access initiatives, including talks on art and children's workshops provided at venues such as hospitals, prisons, libraries, museums, art clubs, schools and regional arts centres. A number of pilot outreach projects are also taking place at libraries in disadvantaged areas of Dublin. Teachers' training courses take place at education centres countrywide.

Education Resources: A series of *NGI Colouring Books* for tiny tots and children; a children's exhibition catalogue, *Children's Art: A Celebration; Artists' Profiles – A Children's Workbook* involving thirty-three contemporary Irish artists; *Exploring Art at the National Gallery*, a handbook for parents, teachers and young people; *Schools' Picture Project*, a series of four posters on Irish Art, and an extensive range of worksheets and activity sheets.

An Education Pack, Information Pack and Transition Year Pack is available free of charge from the Education Department. Write three weeks in advance if you wish to book a tour.

The address of the National Gallery of Ireland is:

Merrion Square West, Dublin 2.
Phone 01-6615133, Fax 6610099.
Email: artgall@tinet.ie
Website: www.nationalgallery.ie

NOTES